My Dream of Stars

My Dream of Stars

From Daughter of Iran to Space Pioneer

Anousheh Ansari

with

Homer Hickam

palgrave
macmillan

The poem by Karen Ravn that appears in the Epilogue is reprinted courtesy of Hallmark Cards, Inc.

MY DREAM OF STARS
Copyright © Anousheh Ansari and Homer Hickam, 2010.
All rights reserved.

First published in 2010 by PALGRAVE MACMILLAN® in the United States—a division of St. Martin's Press LLC, 175 Fifth Avenue, New York, NY 10010.

Where this book is distributed in the UK, Europe and the rest of the world, this is by Palgrave Macmillan, a division of Macmillan Publishers Limited, registered in England, company number 785998, of Houndmills, Basingstoke, Hampshire RG21 6XS.

Palgrave Macmillan is the global academic imprint of the above companies and has companies and representatives throughout the world.

Palgrave® and Macmillan® are registered trademarks in the United States, the United Kingdom, Europe and other countries.

ISBN-13: 978-0-230-61993-7

Library of Congress Cataloging-in-Publication Data
Ansari, Anousheh, 1966–
 My dream of stars : from daughter of Iran to space pioneer / by Anousheh Ansari with Homer Hickam.
    p.   cm.
  ISBN-13: 978-0-230-61993-7 (hardcover)
  ISBN-10: 0-230-61993-2 (hardcover)
  1. Ansari, Anousheh, 1966– 2. Women astronauts—United States—Biography. 3. Astronauts—United States—Biography. 4. Space flight—United States. 5. Iranian Americans—Biography. 6. Muslim women—United States—Biography. 7. Businesswomen—Texas—Biography. 8. Telecommunication—United States. 9. Social entrepreneurship—United States. 10. Iran—Biography. I. Hickam, Homer, 1943– II. Title.
CT275.A736A3   2010
629.450092—dc22
[B]

                                                                            2009025884

A catalogue record of the book is available from the British Library.

Design by Letra Libre, Inc.

First edition: March 2010
10 9 8 7 6 5 4 3 2
Printed in the United States of America.

To Ilya,
whose innocence and purity of love
gives me hope for brighter tomorrows.

"All men have the stars," he answered, "but they are not the same things for different people. For some, who are travelers, the stars are guides. For others they are no more than little lights in the sky. For others, who are scholars, they are problems. For my businessman they were wealth. But all the stars are silent. You—you alone—will have the stars as no one else has them—"

The Little Prince by Antoine de Saint-Exupéry

Contents

Acknowledgments

Writing this book was not easy because I always look to the future rather than back at the past. Reliving tough childhood memories is not something I would do voluntarily so I must thank Homer Hickam for encouraging me (and sometimes harassing me) to finish this book. Otherwise, it would only exist in my head and in my scattered journals.

I decided to tell my story to bring a voice to all the amazing women in the world, especially to Iranian women who have fought and continue to fight for their freedom, and to Iranians around the world who have left their homeland in search of that freedom and better days. It is sometimes difficult to see the true face of a nation when what is prevalent in the media is a hideous image. I hope this book shows readers that there is another side to the beautiful country I left as a teenager and that there are still many Anoushehs who live in Iran with hopes and dreams of a brighter, peaceful future.

My dreams might have never come true without the opportunities that the United States of America afforded me, for which I'm forever grateful. I learned the meaning of freedom in my adopted country and I hope that America continues to symbolize freedom and the land of opportunity to people around the world as it did for me.

I am who I am today because of the unconditional love and support of my mother, Fakhri Shahidi. She, in many ways, portrays the strong will and survivor spirit of the women of Iran. A very special thanks also goes to my sister Atousa Raissyan, who was my "raison d'être" growing up, her beautiful face and soulful eyes always giving me hope no matter how dire the situation.

I would never have been able to start a new life in United States if not for the foresight and guidance of my Aunt Chamsi and Uncle Frank Brown and for that they have my eternal gratitude. I would also like to thank my father, Houshang Raissian, for keeping my mind open to all the possibilities that life holds for us. A personal note of gratitude is due to my father-in-law, Hosein Ansari, for being like a second father to me and, of course, to Amir Ansari for being a true friend and a brother. Our bond is stronger than blood.

My life took a course correction toward the space station on the day I met Peter Diamandis and I'm eternally grateful for his contagious passion and pure friendship. Of course, it was Space Adventures and its president, Eric Anderson, who made my trip possible and I cannot thank him and all the Space Adventures support team enough.

I would also like to thank Michael Lopez-Alegria and Mikhail Tyurin, my crewmates, for taking me to my home amongst the stars and Jeffry Williams and Pavel Vinogradoff for returning me home, safe and sound, to my family. My trip would not have been possible without the support of the Russian Space Agency and NASA. I admire all the great men and women who work at both of these agencies for their passion and dedication to space exploration.

Finally, I would not be where I am today without the true love and support of my soulmate, Hamid Ansari. He is not only my husband but also my mentor, best friend, and source of energy. I cannot imagine what my life would be like had I not met and married him. Without his resilience and enthusiasm, my dream of stars would have remained just that, a dream. With him, all my dreams, past, present, and future, can come true.

Preface

Call this a love story that ends not only with an embrace but a fortune gained, a dream fulfilled, and a voyage to the far and magnificent reaches of space. After everything was done and I landed beneath silky parachutes on the high desert of Kazakhstan, I realized it wasn't rocket engines that had propelled me to the stars but the infinite power of hopes, dreams, and especially love, which transcends everything, even the universal principles of physics.

Wherever I go, I am asked to tell the story of how I flew into space. I am pleased to tell it, yet I fear my words are inadequate to explain the passion, the joy, and sometimes the despair I experienced during every stage of the journey it took to get there from my youth in Iran.

I recall watching from the International Space Station the glow of the sun as it began its rise. From my vantage point 220 miles high, I could see the glimmering threads of gold and silver along the edge of our magnificent planet that heralded a new tomorrow. I found myself delighted not only with this glorious apparition, but with all the new tomorrows coming at me, one after the other as I raced around the world, safe inside my aluminum cocoon. When I was in space, I felt free of all the trivial details that can preoccupy the minds of humanity daily. I had been blessed to not only dream of the stars but also to be visiting them. But even in space, I was aware that the light of our tomorrows is sometimes threatened by the darkness of our yesterdays.

><>*<

Although beautiful in its own way, I did not enjoy seeing the sun draw a deep shadow across the planet, snuffing out continents and seas alike. As far as I was concerned, that encroaching darkness represented yesterday. Although some say that one's past is the primary predictor of one's future, I firmly believe this is not the case—our yesterdays are gone, done, and finished. Only what we do now to make our tomorrows better is important.

><>*<

Rockets that go into deep space use stacked engines called stages. As each stage is exhausted, it is detached and left behind while the next one blazes higher. Just as I once rode a multistaged rocket into space, I invite you to take this journey with me through the stages of my life, propelled not by rocket fuel but by determination, perseverance, and the power of that sweetest energy of all: love.

My Dream of Stars

First Stage

An Iranian Girl

Growing Up Iranian

*T*he music stopped playing and was replaced by an announcement. "All systems ready—initiating countdown. *Deseyit* (ten), *Devyit* (nine), *Vocem* (eight) . . ." *I can't believe I am here. Is this really happening? Am I really soon going to be floating in the weightlessness of space? Is this real? Or am I in the dream I had as a little girl in Iran? So much has happened since I left there as a teenager, so many wonderful and happy things, and so many tragic things, too. But no matter. The rocket beneath me is stirring alive, just as my mind is alive with the dreams and memories of that Iranian girl whose blood courses with the history of an ancient land . . .*

⁂

On a beautiful starry night, in a small hospital in the city of Mashhad in the country of Iran, my life began as the first child to a loving family. I am now Anousheh Raissyan Ansari, a citizen of the United States of America, whose blood courses with the glory and traditions of ancient Persia and modern Iran. Raissyan is the surname of my father, and Ansari that of my husband. Anousheh is Persian for "eternal." I like to think my name reflects the hopes and dreams of my parents for my future.

My Iranian roots go back for as long as anyone can know such things. I was born in 1966 in the Iranian holy city of Mashhad, a metropolis of parks and mosques nestled in the valley of the Nashaf River. All I have of it now are my memories. When I glimpsed the old city from space, a perspective too high to allow much detail, Mashhad appeared quiet and peaceful, and I hope it is. In ancient times, Mashhad was the home of great mathematicians, astronomers, and scientists. Perhaps I am so attracted to the cosmos because I was born in this city of science. I often think of its people, just as I think of my parents and the happiness they experienced when they lived there.

My mother is Fakhri Shahidi, the fourth child among six brothers and sisters. The Shahidi family is known for its long line of Mashhad holy men and for its charity. To help feed the poor, several times a year the Shahidis held an elaborate prayer ceremony called *sofreh* (which literally means "tablecloth"). On *sofreh* days, the delicious aroma of cooking food emanated from giant copper pots atop a bonfire in my grandparents' yard, signaling to everyone that a feast for all who were hungry was being prepared. Sometimes, as many as a thousand people came to be fed, the food set out on white sheets on the floors of the many rooms of the old Shahidi house.

I was four years old when I attended my first Shahidi *sofreh.* My mother and I were greeted by my grandmother, a short, solid woman with thin legs showing from beneath her white chador, the long robe worn by traditional Muslim women. After a word to her daughter, she took me by my hand to show me something she thought I would like. "Look there, Anousheh," she said, and I followed her pointing finger with big, curious eyes to the wall where huge green and black tapestries hung like giant flags. On them were scenes of battles and messages I could not yet read. "Those are words from our holy book, the Koran," Grandmother Shahidi explained. "Those men were knights, the descendants of our prophet, Mohammed. They sacrificed their lives for us in the old battles."

Even then, I had a reputation for asking lots of questions, but before I could think of one, I was distracted by some cookies on a tray. I made a grab for one, but my grandmother snatched my hand away, saying, "No, Anousheh, it is wrong to eat from the *sofreh* until after the prayer. Even if no one sees you, God will know." She then dispatched me with, "I believe your mother is looking for you."

I sprinted from the room and called for my mom, finding her in the courtyard with some other women. I went to her, hung onto her hand, and told her I was hungry. As a child, all my relatives knew that when I got something in my head, it was almost impossible to distract me. Mom cut short her conversation with the women and led me to one of the rooms. She told me to sit down beside her. "No fidgeting," she said. "We will be eating soon. Do you hear me, Anousheh?"

I heard her well enough and, though I had great difficulty doing it, I forced myself to sit quietly. After a few minutes, I grew bored and began playing with Mom's chador, clutching a corner of it and pulling it over my head to pretend I was a great explorer in a cave. Mom uncovered me and ordered me to start behaving like a lady. It wasn't the first time I'd heard this admonition. From what I could gather, any fun activity like running or climbing a tree was not for ladies. Boring stuff, like playing with dolls or kitchen toys, was all a lady was allowed to do. I kept telling myself if I had been a boy, life would have been so much more fun!

Throughout the rest of the day, I peppered Mom with questions about the *sofreh*. Most of all, I wanted to know why were my grandparents feeding all those people? Mom explained that people who are blessed with abundance have a duty to help those who are less fortunate. As good Muslims, my grandparents had a duty to share their blessings with those in need. I liked that answer and was proud of my grandparents. I have never forgotten their example, either. Everything I have, I worked very hard to attain, but I still recognize the need to give back in every way I can.

That night in bed, still excited by all I had learned at the *sofreh,* I eagerly looked forward to the next day when I could ask more questions of my weary mother. *How do birds fly, Mom? Why don't we have wings? Why do stars twinkle? Why are my eyes brown? Why do trees die in the winter? Why is the snow white? Why are you looking at me like that?* I was happy when I thought up questions and happier still when Mom provided me with answers—although perhaps there is some doubt as to whether this made her as happy as her precocious child.

My mother was petite, with flowing ebony hair and dark, sweet eyes. As a young man, my father was handsome, strong, and solid, with a square chin and piercing eyes. People called my parents the Romeo and Juliet of Mashhad. But just as trouble found the original Romeo and Juliet, so it would find this loving young couple—terrible trouble that would devastate our family.

Although he is Papa to me, my father's true name is Houshang Raissyan, the eldest of three children in a proud family of prosperous merchants. Before the troubles came to us and long before I was born, Grandfather Raissyan—I called him my *Buhbuh*—was the son of a very rich man. As befitted his status, my tall and handsome grandfather always wore the latest Western fashions. My Grandmother Raissyan, whom I called my *Maman,* told me stories of how he strutted in the bazaar, carrying a marvelous cane with a little light on the end that turned on and off each time he tapped it on the ground. Only fifteen at the time of their arranged marriage, Maman was an innocent young woman who had no idea what marriage meant. When she moved into her new house as a married woman, she carried with her a trunk full of dolls to play with.

Soon after their marriage, Buhbuh's father, in a stray remark to the wrong person, insulted the Reza Shah, and the vengeful dictator took everything from the Raissyan family. To make ends meet, Buhbuh became a veterinarian, ironically for the shah's government, journeying to remote villages to vaccinate livestock and educating villagers about the techniques of modern animal husbandry. Suddenly finding herself married to an ordinary government worker and with a baby on the way, Maman grew up quickly.

Though I loved them both, I confess I worshiped my Buhbuh. He made up riddles and was delighted when I quickly solved them. "You are a smart girl, Anousheh," he would tell me. I wanted to be even smarter, just for him.

During the first four years of my life, my parents and I lived in a comfortable little house in Mashhad with a lovely garden and a large balcony with a wall of brightly colored tiles with the image of a swan. Both sets of grandparents lived nearby. I was very happy and everyone doted on me. Perhaps I was even a little spoiled. Contented child that I was, I could not imagine any of the terrible problems coming our way.

✣✣✣

Most of the nights when I looked down from space, I saw vast thunderstorms. I knew it must be unpleasant for those experiencing the storms on the ground, but from hundreds of miles above, the storms were a glorious and magnificent light show. One night, as I was listening to Johann Pachelbel's *Canon in D Major* on my iPod, it looked as if someone was orchestrating the lightning in perfect coordination with the majestic music. At first I was enchanted, but then I realized I was watching the tumult from a peaceful platform far overhead, much as God must watch our travails on Earth from above. So often as a child, I envied Him this view and wished for the ability to soar above the heartbreak that struck my family like bolts of lightning and peals of thunder.

✣✣✣

When the shahs ruled, compulsory military service was required for all young Iranian men. After Papa served, mostly in the capital city of Tehran, he came back to Mashhad and began working in a print shop. The work was not very interesting to him, so one day he came home and surprised my mother with the announcement that we were moving to Tehran. His plan was to continue his education so that he could get a better job and build a better future. Though Mom was fearful of such a radical move, her love for Papa was so great that she went along without much argument. Within a few weeks, Papa left for Tehran and Mom and I packed to follow him. Although I was not quite sure why we were moving, it soon became clear that the life I had known in Mashhad was over.

To understand what became of us when we moved to Tehran, it is necessary to understand the political climate of Iran in 1970. At the time, the country was ruled by Mohammad Reza Shah Pahlavi, the son of the man who destroyed my great-grandfather. Many people in Iranian politics considered the shah a puppet of Western powers, particularly the United States and Great Britain. Other Iranians saw him as a steady ruler who kept the country stable and prosperous.

The shah was a cosmopolitan man and reform-minded. He supported what came to be known as the White Revolution, which extended voting rights to women and gave parliamentary representation to farmers and workers. He also campaigned against illiteracy and ruled that secular education institutions were a higher priority than religious schools. Although these reforms were popular with most Iranians, the shah's increased funding for secular education infuriated many Iranian religious leaders. Other groups hated the shah for their own reasons. The shah was so fearful of these enemies that he ruled the country with an iron fist, which, of course, earned him even more enemies. Like most Iranians, my parents and grandparents were apolitical and just wanted to be left alone to work hard and enjoy life.

We moved into an apartment in Tehran and my father enrolled at the university, working odd jobs when he had free time. At first, I missed Mashhad, but eventually I came to love Tehran with all its bustle and excitement. Then, to my delight, my Buhbuh and Maman, unable to bear our absence, came to live with us. Buhbuh quickly found a good job as an accountant for a Caterpillar agricultural equipment dealership owned by one of his old friends. For a while, it seemed we had traded the happiness of living in Mashhad for a new happiness in Tehran.

Also living in our crowded apartment was my uncle Shahram and a housekeeper who had worked for the Raissyan family for decades. She was mute, so we used a special sign language to "talk" to her. Although the housekeeper doted on me, she did not get along with my grandmother. There is a Persian saying: When there are two cooks, the soup is either salty or bland. Now, counting my mom, there was a third cook and they had daily arguments about household management. I learned a lot about forming and defending a position from observing these three opinionated women!

I was five when my sister Atousa was born. Though I loved her instantly, my love was not enough to protect her from the unhappiness that was about to engulf my family like a dark, swollen river. Soon after Atousa's birth, my father came home and declared, "I'm going to America." The tone in his voice was clearly meant to stop debate, but that is impossible in an Iranian family. After persistent questioning from my grandparents, Papa said the idea had come from Mom's brother, who had immigrated to the United States.

"It's the land of opportunity," my father said, quoting his brother-in-law, "and anybody can be rich there." My mother reluctantly agreed and, after a while, my grandparents gave in, too. Papa's plan was to carry Iranian handicrafts and rugs with him and establish a business to sell them. To purchase these goods, we sold everything that was not an absolute necessity. Papa stuffed his bags with the merchandise and promised to send for us when he was settled.

Papa was gone for nearly a year, and during that time I heard little from him except for occasional letters and photographs. His letters mentioned only that he had successfully sold his wares but for very little profit and now he was trying to figure out what to do next. When he returned for a brief visit, he and Mom argued constantly. Mom was clearly miserable when he went back to the States, which in turn made me miserable. To make myself feel better, and also because I loved her so much, I played with my baby sister and held her in my arms as if she were a fragile porcelain figurine. She made me smile even though I was sad.

The next time my father returned, he stayed at a hotel, which seemed very strange to me. Soon Mom, her eyes red from crying, gave me the news. She said, "Your father wants a divorce," and I felt as if my whole world was crumbling. My heart pounded and it was difficult to breathe. Seeing my distress, Mom took me in her arms. "You are a big girl, Anousheh," she told me. "Now you must be very brave for your sister."

Even with Papa gone, my grandparents insisted Mom, Atousa, and I stay with them. This was wonderful since I loved my Bubbuh and Maman so much. One of the really sweet things they did for me was to let me sleep on their balcony, where jasmine, orange, and lemon trees grew in large pots. During the summer, it was also a fragrant, cool escape from the noisy city. Buhbuh fitted a net over my little foldout cot to protect me from mosquitoes, but I always pushed it back because I wanted to see the stars. When they came out, twinkling above the snow-covered peak of Mount Damavand, I would lie there on my cot and let my mind wander, pretending I was up in space. The night sky was not only a playground for my mind, it was also a refuge where I could hide amongst the stars, away from all the sadness in my life.

Perhaps my love of the stars was also inspired by my favorite book, *The Little Prince*. The book is about a pilot whose plane crashes in the desert.

The pilot meets a little boy, a prince, from a distant planet. When the prince begins to talk about how beautiful his planet is, the pilot is entranced. Most people who read the book identify with the pilot, but I identified with the lonely prince who missed his home planet. One part in the book I particularly liked was when the little prince traveled to a planet occupied by a businessman who claimed ownership of all the stars.

"What do you do with them?" the little prince asked, and the businessman answered, "Nothing. I own them."

The reason the prince told the story was because he wanted everyone to know the businessman was wrong. He didn't own the stars at all because he didn't know what they were for. Even as a child, I thought I knew. The stars were a place of escape where nothing was sad and everything was beautiful.

But neither the stars over Mount Damavand or the stories of *The Little Prince* could keep the realities of life away. My mother soon learned that the reason my father wanted a divorce was because he had fallen in love with another woman. Over the next several months, every time he came to visit there was yelling and fighting. Even our mute housekeeper pitched in with bellicose gesticulations. Just wanting it to stop, I fled to the bedroom I shared with my mom and my sister. To this day, if anyone raises their voice, I get nervous and do my best to calm things down. Some say my ability to calm others is my strongest attribute in a meeting. It is a skill I learned the hard way.

In the end, Papa got his divorce and remarried quickly. For many weeks afterward, while I read in the living room, I heard my mother weeping in our bedroom.

I felt like weeping, too. I loved my dad and missed him a lot. When he was around he was good to me and always encouraged me to do well in school. A few months after the divorce, my mom decided she didn't want to stay with my grandparents anymore. Since they were Papa's parents, it was a constant reminder of her failed marriage. Even though it was hard to afford a separate place, she got a second job and eventually found her own tiny apartment close to my grandparents. Our new home was on top of a bank and had only two rooms. There was no kitchen; just a sink, refrigerator, and a small stove, all wedged beneath a stairwell. The larger of the two rooms served as the living and dining room. We slept in the smaller room, all in the same bed. I didn't mind the close quarters, but missed my Buhbuh and Maman and the cool, fragrant balcony where I slept with the stars. In our new apartment, there were no stars, only a noisy portable air-conditioning unit to help us sleep during hot summer nights. Every night, as we lay in bed, Mom held us in her arms. Sometimes, I would touch her cheek and find it wet with tears, and then I would silently weep myself.

Of course, not everything was sad. Before we went to bed, Mom usually turned on a radio program called "Stories of the Night," which was often about Sherlock Holmes. I admired the detective because he had an answer to every question, and came to that answer by dispassionate, deductive reasoning. We also had a tiny television set and I loved to watch American television programs, especially *Star Trek*. I thought Captain Kirk had the best job possible—to boldly go where no man had gone before! Mr. Spock, Captain Kirk's science officer, was much like Sherlock Holmes in that he always had an answer based on logic and reason. Of all the crew of the starship *Enterprise,* I wanted most to be like Spock.

Although Mom had full custody of Atousa and me, my father visited on weekends. He seemed happy because he finally had a good job, vice president of sales for the largest wine company in Iran. One time he drove to the vineyards in a nearby city and took me with him. I was happy because I longed for the loving relationships I'd observed between my friends and their fathers and thought that maybe if we spent those hours driving together, we would become closer. Sadly, it didn't happen. Papa got very ill on the trip so we stopped at a hotel and stayed the night. I became like a little nurse trying to make him comfortable but he told me not to worry. He sent me to the lobby to watch TV while he tried to sleep it off. The next day, even though he was still not feeling well, he took me to a few places for sightseeing but I could see he was miserable. With very little conversation, we drove back to Tehran.

After a while, I began to think we were so distant because I was a girl and he didn't know how to talk to me. I resolved to be more like a boy in order to gain his confidence. If he was carrying a heavy case, I would try to pick it up to show him how strong I was. I played soccer and basketball, and acted tough so he might think me as worthy as a son. But no matter what I did, nothing changed.

Gradually, using the deductive reasoning of Sherlock Holmes and Mr. Spock, I came to a conclusion about my father. He was painfully shy, and that was why he had such difficulty showing emotion. When he was very young, a terrible infection had made him partially deaf. To hear anything at all, he had to wear big hearing aids in both ears. It was easy to imagine the ridicule he must have endured as a boy in school and probably accounted for his tendency toward being an introvert, even with his family.

Though I believed I knew why he was so distant with me, I still longed for Papa's approval and love. During one very special time when I was visiting him, he was drinking a glass of wine, and suddenly his eyes filled with tears. He opened his arms and I fell into them, my head held tight against his chest. I could tell that he was crying but he never uttered a word. We just held onto each other and let our tears come. I cherish that moment still.

Despite all the sadness around me, I was an optimistic child. I had a vivid imagination and often dreamed of being an astronaut, a scientist, or an inventor. My Maman, who was forward-thinking when it came to the independence of women, helped me in this regard. She would always say, "Anousheh, I think you should become a doctor or an engineer."

"Why is that, Maman?"

"Because you have to be the master of your life. You should never have to hold out your hand to your husband. Always be prepared to take care of yourself."

It was good advice, and Mom also promoted it by seeing to the education of her daughters. She enrolled us at Jeanne D'Arc, a French Catholic school known for its academic excellence. Since it was expensive and the child support from Papa was not enough to cover all our bills, Mom was working two jobs. During the day she worked at a university in an administrative office, and at night she was employed in a laboratory doing blood analyses. Her long hours allowed Atousa and me to live a normal life. We never felt poor.

Jeanne D'Arc, an all-girls school, was staffed mostly by nuns. They were tough, those nuns. The first half of the day, we studied our subjects in Farsi, the national language of Iran, and the second half in French. Our annual exams were long and difficult and every class required hours of homework each night plus weekends and holidays.

At Jeanne D'Arc, I began to realize my potential not only for academics but also for physical activities. I became especially close to two of my fellow students, Elham and Soheila. We were called the Three Musketeers and could get rowdy, particularly during recess when we played a game similar to rugby. The rules were simple: protect the ball at all costs. I was deadly serious when I played. I didn't care if my uniform got torn or if I got scratched and bruised. The only thing that mattered was winning. Once, when one of our players was smothered in a pile of fighting girls, she actually passed out. In reaction to this, and multiple other bruises and skinned knees and elbows, the sisters banned our game and confiscated our ball. We went out and got another ball and kept playing. When that ball was also taken away, we rolled one of our jackets into a ball and kept going. The sisters finally gave up.

Of course, sometimes we Musketeers outsmarted ourselves. Hoping to get out of class, we took a sample of sulfuric acid from our chemistry lab and poured some of it in our classroom to make it stink. To our vast disappointment, the teacher came in and didn't even wrinkle up her nose. She just stopped for a second, probably realized what we were up to, and went ahead as if nothing had happened. The joke was on us. We all went home that day with terrible headaches.

There was a big, beautiful Catholic church on the school courtyard. Sometimes, while the Muslim students played outside, Christian students had mass and prayed inside the church. Curious as ever, I always wanted to go inside and look around even though I never felt a need to change my religion. I had Christian friends; I had Jewish friends; I had Muslim friends. The way I saw it, we went to different places to worship the same God. Despite an obvious dedication to their religion, the nuns never tried to convert us, either. They were there to educate us and did a grand job.

I studied three languages at Jeanne D'Arc: French, Farsi, and Arabic. Arabic was the toughest for me, even though I practiced it during my daily prayers. As much as possible, I tried to be an observant Muslim, including fasting at Ramadan. Mom was against this, saying I was too young to fast and that it was bad for my health. I got around her by spending as many nights as possible during Ramadan with my grandfather, who was also fasting. Observing the rules of Ramadan made me feel closer to God, although even as a child I sensed the key to understanding our creator was in my physics, chemistry, biology, and math books. With each new theory or law of nature I learned, I marveled at the harmony and delicate balance of our universe.

Every day after school, Atousa and I visited our grandparents. Usually we were joined by our cousin Arshia, the son of my Uncle Sharam and Aunt Mehdokht. Whenever I got a chance to stay overnight, I always looked forward to sleeping on my grandparents' balcony beneath the stars. There, as the night grew darker and the great constellations formed, I studied them, pondering how the universe started and how it would end. I wondered if I had a special destiny and, if so, how I might discover what it was. "Someday," I promised the stars, "I will visit you and you will tell me all I need to know." It was always such a disappointment when I woke to find the morning had chased them away.

But let me tell you something wonderful about stars.

They are like dreams.

If you look for them, they always come back.

Revolution

I n late 1978, when I was twelve, I started hearing words like *revolution,* *imperialism,* and *communism.* People were demonstrating in the streets and shouting that the shah should abdicate. Since the old shah had taken away all of my great-grandfather's belongings, I thought they were playing a very dangerous game. I didn't know much about the latest shah but his wife, Empress Farah, had gone to Jeanne D'Arc. There was a plaque in her name at the school's basketball court so I thought I had something in common with her. She had also translated a children's book I loved, *Little Mermaid,* by Hans Christian Andersen. Of course, none of this mattered. The great wheel of history was turning against the shah and the empress.

Even in our quiet neighborhood, demonstrators began to appear. I had never seen people so angry. I heard guns being fired and there was news of people being killed. It was scary but, I confess, sometimes also exciting and romantic. Although I had no real passion for politics, there were times I felt a young girl's yearning to join the rebels.

Then something terrible happened. In the city of Abadan, terrorists set fire to a movie theater, and more than 400 people were burned to death. After I read about this, I had horrible nightmares. I loved going to the movies but for a long time afterward, it made me feel claustrophobic. Even though the shah denounced the act and swore he had nothing to do with this atrocity, his regime was blamed and the angry crowds grew even larger. When the demonstrations became especially violent, schools would send word for parents to come and get their children. Since Mom was at work and my grandfather, who'd had a heart attack, was too sick, it was usually up to Maman to come after Atousa and me. Since she didn't drive, Maman had to hire a taxi. Once, when a demonstration was very near our school, Maman arrived sighing and clucking her tongue at the insanity of it all. She threw open the door of the taxi and urged Atousa and me to jump inside. Suddenly, the mob descended on us and started beating on the cab. I was terrified but Maman just stared straight ahead and ordered the driver to go. When the pressure was on, she could be a rock.

I had no concept of revolution, but it was all Iranians talked about. Every day, angry crowds carrying posters of Ayatollah Khomeini marched through the streets, shouting "Death to the shah!" Things got more dangerous when the rebels assaulted military bases and armed themselves. The police and military were losing control. The rule of the shah was coming to an end.

One night, my mother, Atousa, and I were awakened by chanting and gunshots. When we heard the sounds of glass breaking below our bedroom window, we were terrified. The revolutionaries had been setting fire to banks and now were coming after the one beneath our apartment. "Get your shoes!" Mom barked and tossed me a chador. She quickly pulled one over Atousa's head, then over her own. She picked Atousa up and we ran down the stairs. I imagine we looked like three black ghosts as we burst out of the door and ran toward my grandparents' house a couple of blocks away. While Mom muttered prayers under her breath, the crowd milled around us with batons and Molotov cocktails in their hands. They pushed and pulled us but we kept running. Exhausted and terrified, we reached a nearby military hospital, where Mom put Atousa down and started banging on the big iron door with both hands, screaming for help. The guard opened the door slightly and Mom begged him to let us in. He opened it a bit more, and she shoved us through into a courtyard, and followed us in. But after slamming the door shut, the guard began shouting at us, asking us why we were in the streets so late and telling us we could not stay, that it was a military base and he could be fired for letting us in. Mom stood her ground and asked if she could use the phone. Still complaining, he led us into a small office where Mom called my grandparents. It was Maman who gave Mom specific orders. "Stay where you are. Do not move until the demonstrators are gone. Then call and I'll come and get you."

Tired, dirty, and frightened, we huddled in one of the hospital corridors in silence. Believing our apartment was in flames, I wondered how we would ever recover. Where would we get the money? Eventually, the guard checked the street and told us it was clear and that we had to leave immediately or he would throw us out. With no choice, Mom took both our hands and we walked as quickly as we could to my grandparents' apartment, which was just a couple of blocks away. Once there, we rang the doorbell. They came down, held us in their arms, and took us upstairs.

The next morning, Mom and Buhbuh went to see what had happened to our apartment. They came back with good news: There had been a fire, but it had not reached the second floor. Except for some broken windows and the odor of smoke, our apartment was unharmed. We were relieved, but from that moment on, the slightest noise would wake me, and I would be alert the rest of the night.

In February 1979, the shah left the country and Ayatollah Khomeini took over. The newspapers and radio announcements said Iran was now a paradise. I was happy that at least there would be no more demonstrations and gunfire. People in the streets began handing out sweets and placing flowers in the rifles of the shah's soldiers, who were now on the side of the new government.

Although the country was settling down, the years of stress had finally gotten to my poor mother. The severe migraines she had suffered since the divorce were getting worse, and a few times she had to be hospitalized. One day, she told me she needed to go back to Mashhad and look after her father who was recuperating from a car accident. I knew she also needed some quiet time to herself. I agreed that Atousa and I would go live with our father for awhile.

Atousa and I packed the few things we had and Papa came and took us to his apartment. On the ride over, he told us about the arrangements. We were going to have our own room, but the apartment was small and we needed to behave and not damage anything.

Atousa clung to my arm as we entered the tiny apartment. There were only two bedrooms, and ours was only ten square feet. In this cramped, windowless space were a desk and a bed with two mattresses. All this should have made me unhappy, but I was strangely excited by this tiny room. In a way, it represented my first taste of independence.

Atousa and I went to school and did our best to not be any bother to Papa and our stepmother. On the other side of Tehran, the American embassy was overrun by Islamic fundamentalists—the beginning of the long hostage crisis that would ultimately isolate Iran from the world. But in our little room, we were barely aware of it. We had other things to worry about. Every night, we slid one of the mattresses off to the floor, where Atousa usually slept, while I slept on the bed. Since we were used to sleeping with our mom, Atousa was scared and often cried, although she did her best to be a big girl. We were both terrified of the cockroaches that infested the apartment building, so every night, we ritually inspected the bedroom together— under the bed, under the mattresses and pillows; everywhere we could think to look. Then we would wrap ourselves in our blankets and sheets like Egyptian mummies. I held Atousa's hand all night long even though my arm often went completely numb.

Jeanne D'Arc, considered evil and foreign by the Islamic government, was closed down by the authorities after a year, and Atousa and I were assigned to another school. Since most schools in Iran taught English, a language we had never learned, Atousa and I were sent to a school across town where French was part of the curriculum. Because of the heavy traffic in Tehran, we had to leave well before the sun was up to catch the school bus. We soon learned that walking in the dark was quite dangerous.

One morning, as we made our way to the bus stop, stray dogs began to gather until there was a snarling pack at our heels. Suddenly a big black dog lunged at us and Atousa literally climbed up my body, hanging from my neck. I froze. As the growling dogs inched closer, I screamed with all my might and a man rushed outside his home with a bat to fend them off. Once we were safe, he began yelling at us: "Why are you in the street at this hour?" We tried to explain that we were on our way to school but he didn't believe us. Luckily, our bus arrived then and we ran to it and jumped aboard.

Still breathless from the dog attack and the angry man, Atousa and I took our seats. I tried to calm down but it felt as if there was no oxygen in the air. I had never felt so helpless. Willing myself to be calm, I held Atousa close while she snuggled into me. It was then that I realized I could no longer afford to have stars in my eyes. A certain steady resolve began to fill my heart and I felt strong. "I will never allow anything bad to happen to you," I swore to my sister. "Not now. Not ever." I decided at that moment to always fight without fear.

Although my promise to Atousa was sincere, before long, the crowded conditions in my father's apartment caused us to be separated. I stayed with Papa, and Atousa went to live with my grandparents. For many months, my room, with its little bed and desk and cockroaches, was my only refuge from the crushing pain of her absence. Because they were on the other side of the city, I could only visit Atousa on weekends, but I was pleased to find her happy there. Still, without my mom nearby and my sister and grandparents so difficult to visit, I sometimes felt like I was no longer part of the family, just an unwanted castoff, permanently adrift. Although I knew in my heart this wasn't true, I had to fight against these feelings. One discovery of my youth was that whatever was bringing me down the night before was never as overwhelming in the morning. To this day, I remember that and use it to stay calm.

By now, Iran was ruled by an Islamic republic that produced a flurry of restrictive laws, one of them against alcohol. As a result, Iran's domestic wine industry was shut down and my father was out of a job. My stepmother was also pregnant and Papa was terribly worried about how he was going to support his family. It was a miserable time. When the baby was born, a boy named Ideen, I happily accepted babysitting duties. I was willing to do anything to help out.

I was a teenager now and, even in the new Iran, I loved school. Happily, Elham, Soheila, and I were able to stay together, although we Three Musketeers had to adapt to the new strictures placed on us by the government. One requirement was we had to wear the *hijab,* or scarf, that covered our hair. I found the *hijab* incredibly uncomfortable. It was hot and itchy, and was forever slipping out of place. We also had to wear a long raincoat-like garment. The only alternative was a full-length chador that covered us from head to toe. This we completely rejected. For one thing, how could we play basketball in a chador?

With the new government came a new military organization called the Revolutionary Guards. Its members were mostly arrogant teenage boys without much education. I learned not to make eye contact with them. They seemed more than willing to use force against anyone who was not properly respectful to them and the government. Although the Revolutionary Guard walked the streets to enforce the dress code, we teenage girls still managed to create our own fashion. We wore tight, skinny jeans and our *hijabs* were colorful scarves with shoes to match. We were often yelled at and threatened by the boys of the Guard. They reminded me of the poisonous snake in *The Little Prince.* The snake claims to be all-powerful despite the fact that he is small and doesn't have legs or feet. When the little prince asks him why he talks in riddles, the snake cunningly replies, "I solve them all." He does, indeed, with his bite. In the new Iran, the boys with guns were like that poisonous snake.

Isolated, Iran soon found itself at war with one of its powerful neighbors. In 1980, Saddam Hussein, thinking to take advantage of the confused situation in our country, sent Iraqi forces across the border to capture oil-rich provinces. Patriotic by nature, Iranian civilians joined forces and fought back hard. What ensued was eight years of war that resulted in millions of casualties and left many cities in ruins. Iran eventually recaptured most of the occupied territories, but the war ground on relentlessly.

The war affected everyone in many ways. In Tehran, like most cities, there were shortages of food, fuel, and supplies. Everything was rationed and we had to stand in long lines for rice, meat, sugar, and oil for the heaters in our homes. The electricity went out nearly every night so I had to use a kerosene lantern to study and do my homework. When the Iraqi planes attacked, sirens screamed and we scrambled to get to a safe place. At my grandparents' apartment, we ran to the first-floor unit of a nice couple who opened their door to anyone in the building who sought safety. The woman was pregnant and I recall she served us tea while we sat quietly, illuminated by only a few flickering candles. Amid the howling sirens and the thump of bombs, I hugged the children close. I didn't understand why they looked to me for safety, but it gave me courage that they did. I sang to them and told them stories of the stars.

After months of war, the attacks began to seem almost routine. We merely shrugged at the sirens. It took exploding bombs to send us to a shelter. Even then, the men often brought their backgammon sets and played by candlelight. The women talked about which store had what rationed goods and planned a strategic attack for shopping. Some of the conversations were funny in a sad way.

"If you'll take my coupons and get my sugar, I'll pick up tissue paper for you."

"What about heating oil?"

"They don't start selling until the afternoon but if we go there first thing in the morning, we can leave our containers with my sister to watch them. We'll go to the other lines, get our stuff, and be back in plenty of time."

Once I went to the rooftop with friends to watch the antiaircraft rockets. It was like a firework display. It all seemed so surreal, but the exploding bombs meant death and destruction for someone. War, I decided, was truly insane.

⁂

As graduation from high school neared, I started to become more and more concerned about my future. My love for the stars had led me to decide that I wanted to be an astrophysicist. But how would that be possible? The new Iran did not encourage higher education for women.

My chance for academic freedom came unexpectedly. My father called me to his side. "We are going to go to America," he said.

"I'm not going anywhere without Atousa," I replied.

"She is coming, too."

"What about everyone else? I don't want to leave Mom or my Buhbuh and Maman."

"Well, you have to. They can come over later. I'm your father and I will decide what's best for your future."

"But how are we going to live in America? And what about my school?"

"You will live however I live. You will eat the same food and sleep in the same place that I do. We will survive."

"But . . ."

"Anousheh, there is no *but!*"

The move was a possibility only through the foresight of my Aunt Chamsi, my mother's sister, who had married a handsome young American army officer and immigrated to the States. When rumblings of revolution started in Iran, Aunt Chamsi cleverly applied for permanent residency for her sisters, plus me and Atousa. We discovered our applications had been accepted and were in the final stages. Now, all we had to do was pick up our paperwork and travel to the United States.

One major problem, however, was that Aunt Chamsi could not include my father in her application since he was no longer married to my mom. After the revolution and the hostage crisis at the embassy, Iranians were not particularly welcomed in the United States, but since Atousa and I were approved, Papa hoped he might also receive permission to go along with us. Many Iranians had used Germany as a stepping stone to the United States. Papa's sister lived near Frankfurt, and he decided that was where we would go on the first stage of our journey.

That was why, on a sunny day in November 1983, after living through four years of the Islamic Republic of Iran, I sat in an airplane while it taxied for takeoff. I gazed longingly at the distant peak of Mount Damavand and wondered if I would ever see my country again. Then a memory of *The Little Prince* and the flower he left behind on his planet came to mind.

The little prince worried about the flower all the time, but could do nothing to help it because he could not return. Iran was my flower, I realized, and now I was leaving it behind. Like the little prince, all I could do was hope for its safety.

As the wheels of the airplane lifted, I felt a moment of doubt. Would I ever see my mom, my grandparents, or my friends again? Was it right to leave behind everything I had ever known? *Yes,* I told myself. A new life—perhaps a more opportune life—awaited me. I felt a quickening of my blood. I reached up and took off my *hijab*.

Second Stage
A Woman of the World

The Alpha Ansari System

While we waited in Germany for our entry applications to the United States to be processed, we stayed with Papa's sister and her family in a Frankfurt suburb. As transients, Atousa and I were unable to attend school, and our German cousins spoke little Farsi, adding to our sense of isolation. The weather was freezing, and though we longed to play outside as we'd done in Iran, we had no choice but spend most of our time staring out the window into the snow-filled street or at the TV screen.

When we did get outside, we realized we were unwelcome visitors in a country filled with racial tension. One time, when we were on a bus, a group of German teenagers surrounded a young Turkish mother with her child in a stroller and began badgering her. At the next stop they picked up the stroller with the baby inside and took it off the bus, then pushed the mother out behind it. The bus driver never said a word, and when the bus began moving again, the teens laughed and looked around for someone else to harass. Atousa and I sank into our seats. Just as in Iran, I tried to avoid eye contact with these young bullies.

Days, weeks, then months passed with no word from the American embassy on when we would receive final permission to emigrate. This included our so-called green cards, which were necessary for us to work in the United

States. At times someone from the embassy would call to say they wanted to see us, so we'd brave the autobahn with my aunt for the ninety-minute drive. Once there, we usually had to wait for hours, and, invariably, it turned out to be something—such as the proper spelling of our names—that could have been done over the phone. Exhausted and forlorn, we would return and start waiting again.

After a couple of months of frustration, we began going to the embassy every day to press our case. My aunt soon tired of driving us back and forth, so we took the bus. Once there, it was always the same tedious process. First, we passed the stern Marine security guard and entered a long, narrow hallway filled with other hopeful immigrants. Then we sat and waited. An American immigration official sat at the end of the hall behind a closed window, doing his best to avoid looking at us. Frustration and helplessness saturated that hall, and I hated it. To this day, whenever I smell the sweet-sour odor of floor wax, I think of that terrible place.

Every so often, the window scraped open and the official called out a name or names. The people called would jump out of their chairs to hurry to the window. Occasionally, they strutted away with their passports containing the exalted green stamp of acceptance. But other times, I watched their faces crumble as they trudged away with the dreaded red stamp of rejection. Once, an old Iranian man received the red stamp and collapsed on the floor. He and his wife reminded me of my grandparents and I wanted to help but there was nothing I could do. As we watched in horrified silence, the elderly man picked himself up and staggered out, his wife clutching his arm. Then the window at the end of the hall scraped open again, and we all looked up expectantly, hoping to hear our names called with the news that we were finally going to receive the coveted green stamp.

But our names were not called. Day after day after endless day we sat there, miserable and smelling that stinking floor wax. I felt so humiliated and degraded; I thought I would die. I was ready to go back to Iran. If this was what life in America was going to be, I didn't want any part of it.

Finally, one morning, the embassy called and we rushed over. This time, my father said he was sure by the cheerful tone of the man's voice on the telephone that we would receive good news. It was late evening when the official at the end of the hall finally barked my father's name. Papa rushed to the window, handed over his passport, and got it stamped. He looked at the stamp, and his steps back to us were slow and weary. He sat down beside me, put his face in his hands, and sighed.

"What's wrong?" I asked, my heart pounding.

"I have been rejected," he answered. "Not you and your sister. Just me."

"Did they say why?"

"Since the application is in your mom's name, they say I can't use it to get a visa." He shook his head. "I'm really not surprised. This is my life."

My poor father would now have to go back to Iran where he had no job and no prospects. He didn't even have a wife since, in anticipation of his arrival, she had already moved to the United States to stay with her parents. I wanted to hold him, to tell him I loved him, but I didn't. Instead, I sat there silently with my arms around Atousa.

Papa contacted Mom and told her the only choice for my sister and me was to either go back to Iran or for her to come to Germany and take over the process. I was ready to go back but Mom said no, I had to go to America if I wanted to have a good future. A few days later, she joined us in Frankfurt and quickly rented a tiny efficiency apartment that was closer to the embassy than my aunt's place. For the first time in months, with the three of us together again, I was happy, although still quite worried about Papa. Before leaving, he had told me he'd see me in the States. Where he'd gone then, I had no idea.

As weeks passed while the embassy requested more forms and records, Mom's money ran short and we had to look for a cheaper place. Since the local universities were closing for the Christmas holidays, we were able to get a tiny room in one of the dormitories. We moved from one room to another like gypsies. Then, as a pale spring sun began to melt the dirty snow outside, our battle with the embassy finally came to an end. We received our green cards—which, I was surprised to discover, are not actually green. In any case, we had them. The bitter process was over, though the path ahead was uncertain, and we knew virtually nothing of the strange land ahead. No matter. We sensed brighter tomorrows and couldn't wait.

✵

We arrived at John F. Kennedy International Airport in New York on April 1, 1984, and from there took a flight to Washington, D.C., where Aunt Chamsi was waiting for us. I was seventeen years old, wide-eyed, and excited. On the drive to her house, I was astonished at how big and clean everything seemed and the smiling, friendly faces I saw everywhere. Although this first impression of my new country was encouraging, I remained cautious. Over the last few years, I had learned that disappointment was always around the corner.

We moved in with Aunt Chamsi and my Uncle Frank in their comfortable house in the pretty suburb of Springfield, Virginia. We felt welcome immediately. Aunt Chamsi, who dressed and looked like a French model, was kind and attentive. Though my Uncle Frank's Farsi was limited, he had learned Arabic for his job at the Pentagon. It was funny to hear this very American man pronouncing Farsi words in a thick Arabic accent. His full name was Francis W. Brown and he was a lieutenant colonel in the U.S. army. Some days when he went to work, he wore an army uniform, but other times civilian clothes. I was never sure of exactly what he did, but it was fun to imagine Uncle Frank was like James Bond and worked with spy satellites to listen in on the evil plots of people halfway around the world.

One thing that was certain about Uncle Frank was that he adored Aunt Chamsi, and it was an adoration that was returned in full. Even after all the years together, I could see their love for one another in their eyes. Together with their son, Tony, they were the perfect family unit I'd always wanted for myself.

From our arrival, Uncle Frank was adamant that only English be spoken at home. Every time Aunt Chamsi would speak Farsi to us, he would say "Uh-uh, *Khoshgel* ("Beautiful" in Farsi), English only!" My aunt, who understood that he was preparing us for life in the United States, would smile and say, "You're right, dear," and switch to English. His rule was frustrating since I understood so little English, but I did my best. A few days after our arrival, Aunt Chamsi drove Atousa and me to a combined middle and high school called Lake Braddock. She handed me a piece of paper with a list of our classes. I stared at it. "But we don't speak English!" I complained. "Aren't you going inside with us?"

My aunt was sympathetic but stern. "Look, Anousheh, stop worrying! You'll be fine. You're both smart girls and I know you'll figure it out." Then, with a smile and a wave, she drove away.

For a few minutes, we just stood there, Atousa looking at me with her big, black, questioning eyes. Finally, I took her hand and we went inside. Everyone moved so fast around us, it felt like we were walking in slow motion. The American students looked nothing like our uniformed classmates at Jeanne D'Arc. They wore all sorts of clothes with different colors and different styles. I clutched the piece of paper in my hand without a clue as to where to go. I stared at the first line. It said: ESL. I had no idea what that meant.

Suddenly, a woman appeared and began speaking in English to us. Flustered, I replied, "*Parlez-vous français?*"

She held up her hand, indicating we were not to move, and left, returning with another woman who turned out to be a French teacher. I explained my situation and the teacher translated the three mysterious letters on my paper: "English as a Second Language," she said, giving me a little map of the school. She took Atousa's hand and said for me to go on, that she would take care of my sister.

When I got to my ESL class, it was like nothing I had ever seen. Kids sat in their seats facing random directions, chatting, and chewing gum. Some had their feet on the desks and paid no attention to the teacher who, after a few minutes, noticed me. I handed him my paper and he glanced at it, then pointed to an empty seat. I took out my notebook and my pencil and copied what he had written on the board. As if he had never seen anyone do such a thing before, he froze for a second, then smiled. The rest of the students stared at me as if I had violated some secret code of conduct.

As the school year went on, I continued to struggle with English although I usually aced my tests in science and math, to the astonishment of my teachers. Science, of course, has a universal language. When I came home with A-pluses marked on these tests, Uncle Frank and Aunt Chamsi praised me. They made me feel like I could do anything. Uncle Frank also started to talk to me about some serious things. He wanted me to understand and appreciate life in the United States.

"English is your big hurdle right now," he told me. "That's why I've enrolled you in English classes at a community college this summer. But here's what you really need to understand. You are not in Iran any more. You are in a country with a lot of opportunities, but it is up to you to take advantage of them. What you have to do is pretty simple: get through high school with good grades, then apply for a student loan and financial aid to go to college. Here, you don't have to have much money to go as high as you want."

This sounded to me like pure fantasy. "You mean somebody will give me money to go to college?" I asked.

Uncle Frank assured me this was true. He said that many American kids didn't take full advantage of all the opportunities but that people from other countries who were not born with such freedom figured out quickly that the only barriers were those they created themselves. He told me that if I worked hard, I would be amazed how many people would step up to help me succeed. There would be no limits to what I could achieve.

"I promise to work *very* hard, Uncle Frank," I told him, and I meant it. I was energized by his advice and ready to tackle anything. The only thing that slowed me down was a strange new shyness that confused me and was overwhelming at times.

In Iran, I never considered myself timid and unsociable, but in the United States I seemed to turn inward. I spoke in a very low voice and hunched my shoulders to make myself smaller and shorter. Maybe it was my lack of English skills that made me so self-conscious or perhaps it was the humiliation I'd experienced in Germany. Uncle Frank kept at me to stand up straight and to hold my head up. If I spoke in a low voice, he would say, "I can't hear you!" Or he would make up some crazy thing like, "What? You want a big nose?" "No! Uncle Frank!" I would shout, "I like roses!" and then he would smile a triumphant smile. I would smile back. I knew what he was doing.

My first summer in the United States, I took English classes from 8:00 a.m. to 6:00 p.m. I rode my new bike to the community college and gradually began to feel like I was an independent, powerful woman. I stood taller and spoke louder, although I was still uncertain of myself around typical American students, who seemed so loud and overbearing.

In the fall, Atousa went back to middle school and I went to my final year in high school. Even though I was still working to perfect my English, it didn't take me long to realize I was far ahead of most of my fellow students in many of my classes. I had studied chemistry, physics, and calculus in the eighth, ninth, and tenth grades, whereas the American students were just getting to those subjects as electives in high school. I noticed immediately how the teachers seemed almost grateful when any of their students made an effort. I could imagine the Jeanne D'Arc nuns clucking their tongues and shaking their heads at the bored, listless American students slouched in their desks around me. I studied hard and was soon earning straight As.

Even though I did well, I hated high school. The other students never welcomed me, and many made fun of my accent. They mocked anyone who was different. Even though I knew the answers to most of the math and science questions, I never raised my hand for fear of being harassed. If there was a project that required me to present something in front of the class, I would nearly always find a way out of it.

Being in a classroom with boys was also a new experience. Not only did they intimidate me but I was embarrassed by their often lewd comments. It also seemed to me that the presence of boys in the school made the girl students more self-conscious about their looks. Don't get me wrong—teenage girls in Iran are interested in boys and looks too, but I don't think they are as consumed by these things as American high school girls. By their dress and makeup, they looked to me like they were in their mid-twenties. I felt like a little kid around them. Looking back, I can't remember making a single friend of any of those girls. This was probably as much my fault as theirs, but at the time I just couldn't relate.

Because my clothes from Iran were unfashionable, Mom gave me a little money to go shopping. Shopping in the United States was a newfound pleasure. The salesladies were so nice, and I began to feel trendy for the first time in my life. It was all so exciting to create a style for myself. I think I even got some appreciative looks from the high-school boys.

Although Atousa and I were settling into our new lives, Mom wasn't doing as well. To her, America was just too big, too fast, and too different.

My Aunt Chamsi was completely Americanized and tried to help Mom adjust but it was never easy, especially since she didn't speak English. After a little over a year, I wasn't surprised when Mom told me she was going back to Iran. She said there were many things she needed to settle there before she could think about living in the United States. I teared up and asked, "Will you ever come back?"

She held my face with both hands. "You have grown up so fast! What happened to my little girl? Of course, I will come back and soon. But you have to take care of Atousa and listen to your Aunt Chamsi and Uncle Frank. I will call you every week. We won't be that far away, not really."

✦❀❀✦

In 1985, I graduated from high school with a record of academic excellence. By then my father was in Los Angeles with his wife and her family. His journey to America had been incredibly difficult. After a few months of wandering from one country to the next, he journeyed to Haiti and hired a fisherman to ferry him across shark-infested waters to the United States. Though he was caught coming ashore, the federal government gave him temporary political asylum. Papa called me right after he was released and asked if I could help him with his visa. Joyful to just hear his voice, I applied for his permanent residency and he soon received it. I was so proud and happy. My father had managed to make his dream come true with great courage and tenacity.

I was still working on my own dream to become an astrophysicist. Unfortunately, my SAT scores in the verbal section were too low to go to Princeton, my first choice. Instead I enrolled at nearby George Mason University, which at least meant I could stay home and save money. Although George Mason didn't have an astrophysics curriculum, it did have an excellent engineering program. Since it was a growing field, I decided to major in electrical engineering. Uncle Frank approved of my choice, saying it would assure me of a good job upon graduation, which I needed badly.

I was able to get a student loan and other financial aid, but money was still a problem. Uncle Frank and Aunt Chamsi helped as much as they could but I felt uncomfortable accepting their gifts. I began working part-time in the university library and as a waitress in a French restaurant to earn extra money.

My college experience was completely different from high school. The students who went to George Mason actually seemed to want to be there. I would go to classes and then hang out at the student union, where they had a big TV and tables and couches. Sometimes when I had early morning classes, I went there and did my homework or slept on a couch until my next class. There were two other Iranian girls, Layli and Shideh, who were also taking electrical engineering and we sometimes studied together. We weren't as close as I had been with my friends in Iran, but it was good to have something in common with two smart girls.

Halfway through my freshman year, Mom came back, saying she finally had enough of Iran and did not want to live apart from us any longer. With the money she brought from selling her apartment in Tehran, and also with some help from Aunt Chamsi, she bought a town home near George Mason. Once again, Atousa, Mom, and I were together, and we were delighted to watch Atousa grow into a beautiful girl with curly black hair and soulful eyes. She was smart and graduated from high school a year early. Following in my footsteps, she chose to major in electrical engineering and was accepted at George Mason.

Finally, it seemed, our toughest days were behind us. I happily anticipated all that would happen in the days and years ahead. Yet, with all my imagination, I could never have guessed that everything for me would change when I met the Ansari brothers.

My life can be divided into two parts: everything that happened before May 18, 1988, and everything that happened afterward. That was the date I met Hamid Ansari, my future husband.

In space, two large stars that are part of the Alpha Centauri system orbit around one another. I like to think my husband, Hamid, and I are like Alpha Centauri A and B: the two stars are nearly equal, each with their own energy and strength, and each has a stable, compatible orbit. Together, they create a bright light in the sky. Separately, each would be only a pale glow.

Dubious celestial metaphors aside, before I met Hamid, I was a young, determined woman with a single-minded mission to get an education and find a good job. I pushed ahead in my studies at George Mason and graduated with honors in three and a half years. Even before graduating, I had landed a job at MCI Telecommunications. As soon as I learned that MCI paid for college courses, I enrolled at George Washington University to get my master's degree. Little did I know that my supervisor at work would become my husband.

But let me back up a little. When I was a junior at George Mason, I met Amir Ansari, my future brother-in-law. I could tell the story of how Amir and I met and how he changed my life, but he tells it better. Therefore, I will let him have his say. After that, my dear husband Hamid will have his say as well. See what a good sister-in-law and excellent wife I am?

A NOTE FROM AMIR ANSARI

I met Anousheh in 1987, when I was seventeen and she was twenty-one. Like her, my family had left the Iranian Islamic Republic for the

United States. My father worked in the shah's government and, for that reason, the people who brought Khomeini to power were not fans of the Ansaris. Before long most of my friends and co-workers had either been arrested or assassinated. In 1979, we left our home with nothing but the clothes on our backs, headed to the airport in Tehran, and took off for a safer and better future.

I liked this United States place instantly! The first thing I wanted to do was go to college. I graduated from high school when I was only sixteen and immediately enrolled at George Mason University in engineering. Hamid, one of my older brothers, already had a degree in engineering and got a job with MCI Telecommunications. He was barely eighteen when he started working, the youngest full-time engineer there.

Oddly enough, I didn't meet Anousheh in an engineering class. Rather, we met in a Russian literature class. On the first day I noticed this fuzzy-haired, nervous little bundle of energy on the other side of the classroom that just wouldn't stop moving. Everything about this girl was in motion: her head, her feet, her legs—everything! It was like somebody had wound her up too tight, then sat her down at a desk and let her go. I also couldn't help but notice, for all her nervous movement, that she was quite good-looking. She had beautiful olive skin and dark eyes, and she wore bib overalls with straps that made her look like an overgrown kid. She was different, that was for sure. I didn't know at the time that she was Iranian, but I knew she was something. Maybe Spanish or Italian, I thought. Or a whirling dervish! After class was over, she grabbed her books and, without a word to anybody, took off.

I saw her again when I was at the student union, where I'd gone to play pool. When I came out of the game room she was sitting on a couch in front of a big television set. She had her elbows on a table, her hands on her cheeks, and her eyes on the television. Occasionally, she'd glance at a page in the book, then turn it. This was studying? Her head was still bobbing, her curls vibrating.

I talked to a few people and found out she was a straight-A student, and I was pleased to discover she was Iranian. Even though I hadn't said a word to her, I got it in my head that she would be perfect for Hamid and I began plotting ways to get them together. The New Year's celebration of the Persian Club was coming up and I figured that was my opportunity. In Iran, it is tradition that thirteen days after the New Year, everybody goes out for a picnic. I made sure both Anousheh and Hamid attended.

As the picnic got going, I started squirting everybody with a water pistol. All the girls ran away except Anousheh. Instead, she came after me with a big water cannon and drenched me! I thought, This is one cool girl! I just had to get her together with Hamid, but before I could make the proper introductions, she was gone.

I was now completely convinced that Hamid and Anousheh needed to be together. I started to hold more parties, inviting them each time. Before this, I was known as a bookworm. Now, I became a party animal! Anousheh was nearing graduation and I was afraid she might take a job somewhere else and Hamid would lose her. I told her there was an opening as a summer co-op at MCI, where one of my brothers happened to work, and that if she got a job there, it would also pay for her master's degree. She thought that was a great idea and I arranged an interview with Hamid.

There is nothing easy about Hamid, and he put Anousheh through a tough interview process. Thank goodness Anousheh impressed him and everybody else at MCI. She was hired and, just as I had promised, MCI agreed to help her get her master's degree at George Washington University. I had finally gotten Hamid and Anousheh together long enough for magic to happen and, to my relief, it worked. Pretty soon, they were dating and, after a few years, they were married. Hamid got a great wife and I got a great sister-in-law.

✧⁓⁂⁓✧

A NOTE FROM HAMID ANSARI

I know Amir's story. I have heard it many times. It's funny the way he tells it and there is even some truth to it. As soon as I met Anousheh, I knew we were meant to be together. Perhaps without realizing it, I had been looking for someone just like her, a woman who would join me to create a powerful team.

After we'd been going out for more than two years, Anousheh and I were scheduled to go to Hawaii on a business trip. Hawaii was so romantic, and I was certain it would be the perfect place for me to propose. I bought a Precious Moments figurine of a boy proposing to his girlfriend. In his hand was a piece of paper with two check boxes, one with "Yes" and one with "No."

After dinner one night we took a walk on Waikiki Beach and sat on a bench to enjoy the moonlight. I had the figurine wrapped in a towel. I gave it to her and said, "Here's a message for you." Then, I handed her a pen. My heart was pounding, my palms were sweating, and my mouth was dry. I think it was the most nervous I had been since I boarded the plane in Iran to come to the States.

My voice shaky, I said, "Check off the one you like." To my relief, and without hesitation, she checked "Yes" and threw her arms around me. I had never thought much about marriage or having a wife, but Anousheh changed all that. Before we were together, I never understood what it was to be complete.

We were married three times. The official date was January 28, 1991, in a Washington, D.C., mosque for Anousheh's maternal grandmother, who came all the way from Iran to see us get married the old fashioned way. But the real date of our marriage is a civil ceremony on January 26, 1991, conducted by a justice of the peace—we just couldn't wait. We got married again on May 26, 1991, in a Persian ceremony with all our friends in attendance. I'm still a little confused about the date of our anniversary, so I play it safe by getting Anousheh gifts on all three occasions!

That was how the Ansari brothers came into my life forever. I am grateful to Amir for his perseverance, but Hamid claims all those parties weren't necessary to get us together. From the moment we met, he says, he knew we were going to get married.

Hamid and I began our marriage believing we could do anything together. We had become citizens of our adopted homeland, we had great jobs with MCI, and I had just completed my master's degree in electrical engineering at George Washington. We felt poised for success. Hamid had committed himself to becoming a millionaire by age thirty and I was intent on helping him reach his goal. It's not that we wanted to spend a lot of money on frivolous things; rather, we wanted the freedom that financial security represented. We also intended to help our families and maybe, if we made enough, help others in need, just as my grandparents had helped feed the poor back in Mashhad.

But trouble came, as it always does. When MCI announced they were closing their Virginia offices and moving to Texas, Hamid, Amir, and I were left in a bind—by then we were all working for the company. Although we were told we could keep our jobs by moving with the company, we refused to leave our families behind. At the time, we were living in a big four-bedroom house with an equally big mortgage. Even before we lost our jobs, we didn't have the money to buy anything other than the most basic pieces of furniture. The walls were bare of pictures and there were no drapes or curtains. When Hamid worried about the wide open windows, I told him I liked it that way since it made the house so bright. I think he almost believed me.

To save money, Amir and my father-in-law lived with us. Even with our combined incomes, it was hard to make the mortgage. After MCI let us all go, it was impossible. One day after seeing Hamid hunched over the bills, trying to figure out how to pay them, I told him, "We can sell this house and go back to living in an apartment. As long as I'm with you, it doesn't matter where we live."

Hamid smiled up at me. "We are not going to sell our house. It is our path to success."

"What do you mean?" I demanded.

"Well, we will succeed because we have to pay the mortgage. Don't you see?"

I loved this man, his optimistic nature, his persistence, and his drive. I went along and we stayed in our big, expensive house with no curtains and little furniture. Then I found a job as an engineer with COMSAT, the Communications Satellite Corporation, which managed communications satellites. Within a few weeks, I was able to help Amir get a job there as well. Just as Hamid had so confidently predicted, the mortgage got paid.

After leaving MCI, Hamid wanted to push forward on his ambition of becoming a millionaire before age thirty. He tried a few entrepreneurial get-rich-quick schemes that looked good on paper but proved to be impractical. Meanwhile, he started a used-car business to bring in some supplemental income. This required us to go to car auctions and trudge past rows of old junkers, looking for ones in reasonably good condition that we could fix up and sell. The auctions were in some of the worst neighborhoods in Baltimore and Washington, D.C., and held inside old garages pumped full of carbon monoxide. After breathing the foul air all day, I usually returned home with a splitting headache. No matter how early we got there, the large dealers always got the best cars and all we got were the leftovers. Once, we opened the trunk of a car and found it full of maggot-infested rotten food. I staggered backward, my hands clamped over my nose and mouth. Still, we scrubbed that car clean.

We kept going, week after week, car after filthy car. Amir joined us sometimes and the three of us would wash and scrub all day. After we detailed each one, we advertised it in the paper. Amir, a natural salesman, was the best at making deals. He answered all the calls and showed our customers the cars. It was always exciting when we made a deal and our customer drove away happy, never suspecting how foul his ride had been just a few days before. The evidence was in our raw, chapped hands, our aching backs, and my throbbing temples.

One hot, muggy summer evening, Hamid and I were washing a car so encrusted with dirt it had taken hours just to get down to the paint. This was the third car of the day. We were both tired, and our hands were red and sore. Suddenly Hamid straightened up, jammed his fist into the small of his back, and announced, "This is stupid!" He threw down his sponge and I saw his eyes were wounded and tired. "We're never going to get this car clean enough to sell. The hell with this business!"

I was holding a water hose in one hand, a sponge in the other. Hamid started to stalk away but I called after him in my sweetest voice. "Hamid?"

He turned toward me and petulantly demanded, "What?"

I turned the hose on him, spraying him in the face, and began to chase him with it. Soon we were yelling and giggling like schoolchildren. After taking the hose from me and soaking me from head to toe, my husband held me, his eyes now alight with happiness. "You're crazy, you know that?" he asked.

"Yes!" I giggled. "Crazy about you!" Then I planted a kiss on his wet cheeks. "Let's finish this and get a pizza."

Although we cleaned that car and made it sparkle, we knew we weren't really getting anywhere. We needed a new plan. But what?

Our social life centered around our family, many of whom lived nearby. Jamshid, Hamid's older brother, was married to Fariba, a lovely Iranian woman, and they had two beautiful little girls, Beeta and Tara, who were also flower girls at my wedding ceremony. On my side of the family, Atousa, finishing her degree in engineering, was living with my mom in a nice town home just a few miles away from our house.

On Sundays everyone came over for dinner. Usually my father-in-law prepared his famous barbeque called *chelo kabab,* which featured long grain, aromatic basmati rice, and tender kebabs. Although his name is Hosein Ansari, I called him my *Baba Joon,* which means "dearest dad" in Farsi. He was indeed dear to me. When his first wife died, his boys were still very young. But Baba Joon managed to raise them successfully and teach them to be brave, self-sufficient, and righteous. Although he was forced to leave behind everything he owned in Iran, he did his best to support his sons, including learning how to cook for them.

To prepare for our feast on Sundays, Baba Joon shopped for the best meat at the best price. Then he spent all morning filleting and cutting the meat into strips and marinating it with seasoning and olive oil before putting it on the grill. Raw, sweet onions; fresh basil and mint; and his famous home-baked bread were served, and also *doogh,* a salty yogurt drink popular with Iranians. Everything was served just as if we were in a gourmet restaurant. The delicious aroma coming from our kitchen when Baba Joon was cooking was almost enough to make us think we were back in Iran. Though we had a dining-room table, we sat lotus-style around a tablecloth on the floor, just as if we were at a *sofreh.* For dessert, there was cool watermelon, hot tea, and, Hamid's favorite, cream puffs. After the meal, we cleared the dishes and stretched out on the floor, our stomachs tight as drums. I think now, *Oh, those were such sweet days!* We were rich in ways that had nothing to do with money.

From the moment we met, my brother-in-law Amir has been very special to me. Like all siblings, we sometimes argue and yell, but minutes later we are best friends again. We first connected through our shared love of space. Amir is even a bigger *Star Trek* fan than I am. He even dangled starship models in his room at our house on a sophisticated system of pulleys and fish lines. He enjoyed making them move like they were flying or fighting. I thought he was crazy in the best kind of way. A typical "conversation" between us went like this:

"Someday I'm going into space, Amir."

"Me, too. But you will go first."

"Why do you say that?"

"I just know it. I know everything."

"Do you know you are sometimes an idiot?"

"Yes, but only when I pay attention to you!"

I was overjoyed when Hamid, after months of looking, finally found a position as the business development manager for an international consulting company. Now that we had some financial security, Hamid decided Amir should quit his job at COMSAT and move to Texas for a temporary consulting job with MCI. Hamid told him, "You can go there for a year or so and come back a smarter and richer man."

At the time, Amir was twenty-one years old and had never lived by himself. Although usually he did what Hamid wanted him to do, now he resisted. "Look, I don't know anybody in Texas," he complained as we gathered around the Sunday *sofreh*. "And since this job at MCI is only temporary, I wouldn't even have my own place. I'd have to live in a hotel."

Hamid answered with the full authority of an Iranian older brother. "It will be good for you and it will be good for us. So what if you live in a hotel? Hotels are nice and you don't have to take care of anything, just work day and night. Think of all the money you would save."

Amir still hesitated. Hamid knew what to say to get him to go. "Amir, your family needs you to do this." Sure enough, Amir moved to Texas. There, just as his older brother had predicted, he met people, networked in the burgeoning telecommunications industry in Texas, and soon became the resident expert in his organization. Still, his phone calls told us he was lonely and homesick. We tried to visit him often and cheer him up, but it wasn't enough.

When I thought about Amir's sacrifice, I decided it was not fair for us to expect him to stay there by himself. One day, I asked Hamid, "Why are we still here? I think we should go to Texas."

Hamid was surprised. "What about your mother and Atousa? You'd be a long way from them."

By then, Atousa had graduated and found a good job. Mom had settled into her new life. It was time to go. When Hamid realized I had made up my mind, he called his boss and told him he was expanding his operation to Texas. In June 1992, Hamid and I packed our bags and moved to a place where, if the tomorrows awaiting us were not better, we knew at least they would be different.

Texas

We moved to Richardson, a small city north of Dallas, where Hamid quickly found me a position as a consultant with our old employer, MCI. It was good to be back with the company again; I liked the people I worked with and made good money. Because Baba Joon stayed behind in our house in Virginia, we continued to pay off our mortgage while renting an apartment. To help out, Amir moved from his hotel and came to live with us. The space was small, but we spent so much time working that we barely noticed. We felt we were poised for a future that was like everything in Texas: bigger and better.

In the early 1990s, there was a palpable sense of optimism in the Texas air. Like MCI, a growing number of companies were moving their operations there, and the area was getting to be known as the Telecom Corridor. Thousands of young, enthusiastic men and women poured almost daily into Dallas, Richardson, and Plano, towns on the central Texas prairie that were growing exponentially in order to support these modern pioneers. Taxes, governmental bureaucracies, rules, and regulations all were kept to a minimum by savvy state and local politicians. But problems began to surface—big problems that threatened our new life.

Hamid's job was to recruit consultants and then hire them out to telecommunications companies for a fee. He had one golden rule: his employees had to be paid, no matter what. But when his client companies were late in their payments and his boss refused to meet the payroll, Hamid was forced to use our own money to cover the shortfalls. When a crunch came, and a number of companies fell behind, Hamid turned to credit cards to meet the payroll, hoping it would be a temporary situation. It wasn't. It was ironic, really—our credit cards were supporting the cash flow of multibillion dollar companies, and the more successful we were, the bigger the problem got. Soon, the credit cards were the only thing keeping his business afloat. We were on the slippery slope to insolvency and everything was going down with us.

So it was, on a Sunday in the fall of 1993, that we met in Hamid's office to figure out what to do. While Amir stood at a whiteboard, ready to write down any good idea, we found ourselves mostly just griping about the unfairness of it all. I added my two cents, saying, "We're financing somebody else's company with our own money. It's crazy!"

"Any other good ideas?" Amir asked with a little smirk. His pen was poised, his white board pristine. He looked expectantly at Hamid and then at me.

Finally, I couldn't stand it any longer. An idea had been building inside me for quite some time. "We should start our own company!" I said with conviction.

I think Amir was already thinking the same thing. "Anousheh is right," he said. "Let's go out on our own." He wrote it down, his felt-tipped pen squeaking on the whiteboard. *Squeak, squeak, squeak,* and there it was, in bright red on white: *Start our own company.*

Hamid stared at Amir's whiteboard and my big idea. Then he shook his head and said, "Maybe some time in the future, but not now. We're broke. How would we pay our employees?"

I said we'd do it the same way we were already doing it, except we wouldn't have to give anything to Hamid's absentee boss. "We all have college degrees," I added. "We work harder than anyone we know. We can do this."

"Yes, we have college degrees," Hamid replied, "but in engineering, not business. And, yes, we're hard workers, but what do we know about business? I think our present situation speaks for itself."

Amir said, "Look. I agree it's risky, but if the worst should happen, we could live *nan va piaz*."

Nan va piaz is an ancient Persian expression literally meaning "bread and onions." The story goes something like this: Back in ancient times, during the invasion of Persia by Arabs, a lone fighter began a resistance movement with only the most basic resources. The movement grew as he won battle after battle. Finally, he chased the enemy army to a city that was their last refuge. On the eve of the big battle, the enemy general sent a message to this Persian hero with a convoy of gold and jewels and also a message that said, "I will give you all my gold and power, but spare my city and allow me to have my kingdom. Do not attack me."

To that, our hero responded by sending all the gold and jewels back with an additional item: a small bag containing an onion and a loaf of bread. He included a note which said, "You have pillaged my country for years and you dare to send me gold and jewels? Tomorrow I am going to attack you. If I win, I will take *all* that you took from us and everything else that you have. If I lose, I will happily go back to where I started, with nothing more than an onion and bread."

Amir's use of the expression resonated deeply with us.

"Do you think you can do that, Amir?" Hamid asked. "Risk complete failure?"

"Is it any different from what we're doing now?"

"Please, Hamid," I said. "Let's do this."

Amir and I waited for Hamid to decide. We knew we could do nothing without him. He was the driving force behind our combined mechanism. He lowered his chin into his hands, his fingers stroking his goatee. I could almost see his mind working, calculating, weighing all the options and the odds. The silence was deafening.

"Hamid," I said, "this is our only chance and we have to do it. You have to trust me!" I took a deep breath and added, jokingly, "Anyway, either go with us or we will be your competition." Of course, my threat was empty and Hamid knew it, but I continued, saying, "You have never been one to play it safe. You have always taken big risks in your life. Take a chance on me—take a chance on us."

I stared into his eyes. They burned into mine and I realized I was clutching my hands tightly together in my lap. I waited until his face slowly softened. "All right," he said at last. He got that look in his eyes, the one that told me he had figured everything out. "Here is what we will do," he said.

Hamid said he would give his boss notice immediately, then see to our incorporation and begin the hiring process. We would get some working capital by selling the stock options we had accumulated as part of our retirement plans at MCI. Amir and I would continue to work as consultants, putting every penny of our salaries left after food and rent into our new company. "You will be our CEO," Hamid said, looking at me. "There is an advantage to having you in that position."

I swelled with pride until Hamid went on to say, "I think maybe there are loans we can get with a woman in charge." Seeing my frown, he added, "You're also detail-oriented. You can keep everything together better than any of us."

Hamid's dark eyes bored into me and Amir. "Listen, you two. This won't be easy. You'd both better be ready for bread and onions!"

Amir and I were so excited we were practically dancing. We decided to call our bright, shiny new company telecom technologies, incorporated, or tti. We used lower case letters just to be different. The first task we set about doing was designing a cool logo, even though there were more important things we needed to do. We were blissfully ignorant about what goes into starting a business.

Our company began as a consulting firm that provided expert engineers to the booming Texas telecom industry. But what followed was a surprise. When I suggested we form our own company, I had no idea of the years of seven-day workweeks and fourteen-hour workdays that would be required. Our life became work and our work became our life. From the moment we opened our eyes in the morning to the time we closed them at night, we struggled to build our company. All the while, Amir and I were still consulting on our own. There was no such thing as a weekend of rest. We took pleasure in simple things, like stopping long enough to watch a Texas sunset. Not only were they beautiful, they were free!

Unfortunately, we soon had to face the fact that, even with all our hard work and countless hours, there was more cash going out of tti than coming in. We paid ourselves nothing but just couldn't seem to get ahead. On paper we were making money, but our bank account was empty. Just as before, the companies to whom we provided consultants fell behind in their payments to us. Hamid became an expert in paying one credit card with another or taking advantage of credit card offers for balance transfers, allowing us to skip one or two months of payments. It kept tti going but pushed us ever deeper into debt.

I began to become concerned about Hamid's health. I watched him every week as he lined up credit card bills on his desk and shuffled them around, worry lines written on his face. There were many sleepless nights for Amir and me, too. We were being ground down.

Eventually we reached the day when we had maxed out every credit card, and there was no one left in the family we could tap. The facts were stark. The payroll was due and we had no money to meet it.

"Is this the end?" I asked Hamid.

"Not yet; have faith," he said.

"What are we going to do?"

Hamid told me his plan. He was going to call one of our credit card companies and ask for an increase on our limit, no matter that we had just gotten one and were supposed to wait a month before asking again.

"Why would they help us?" I wondered.

Hamid looked at me, trying to appear confident. "What's the worst thing that could happen?" he finally asked.

I smiled tenderly at this man I loved. "*Nan va piaz!*" I practically shouted. The credit card company heard him out, then put him on hold. Hamid bit his lip and waited on the phone while I nervously paced up and down the corridor, feeling my heart pound wildly. I started saying prayers under my breath and promised God I would be forever in His debt if He helped us. After what seemed like an eternity, the representative came back on the line and told us our increase was approved. I was so excited I wanted to scream. The furrow on Hamid's forehead disappeared.

We had survived one more day.

There would be other days like that one but, somehow the weeks passed, then months, and we were still in business. With each close financial call, I saw the need to learn more about how to run a business. I began reading books and taking classes in finance at a nearby community college, where I learned about the possibility of applying for small business loans. I marched into a bank, sat down before a loan officer at a big desk, looked him in the eye, and asked for $200,000. After reviewing our records, he agreed to give us half. We were elated. We began to think about a product line of our own and started looking for investors.

One day, a rich man came to my office. He was very "old Texas"—I could almost smell the sagebrush and oil on his boots. With a flourish, he took off his big hat and sprawled on a chair in our tiny conference room. While I gave my pitch on how tti was an up-and-coming company with a bright future, he cocked his big, bushy eyebrows and peered at me, his eyes like hard blue marbles.

After I finished, he spoke. "Little lady," he drawled in a voice that sounded like vast plains and dry holes and persistence and sudden wealth. "I'm gonna do ya'll a big favor. I'm not gonna invest one thin dime in your company."

I was a bit startled. "I don't understand."

He stood up. "I think you and your I-ranian boys are gonna be a big success. Ya'll gonna make a lot of money, and that means ya'll don't want to have a buncha little ol' investors like me asking for their piece of the pie. My advice? Keep it all to yourselves."

The man put on his cowboy hat and made his way out. Hamid and I sat there, more than a little stunned. Finally, Hamid muttered in disbelief, "I guess he sees something in us that we don't."

"Maybe we're better than we think we are," was my reply.

I could tell by Hamid's expression that he didn't understand. Neither did I, but we were both about to learn a lesson on what can be accomplished with perseverance in the face of adversity.

<hr/>

Hamid and I regularly left for the office before sunrise and returned long after the sun had set below the flat Texas horizon. Usually, all we managed to eat was a quick microwave dinner while watching classic *Star Trek* reruns or *Star Trek: The Next Generation.* Then we turned to our laptops to work some more before going to bed. We used to laugh and say the neighbors must think they were living next door to the Addams Family, the way we prowled around at night. When I was outside at night, I always stopped to glance up at my oldest friends—the stars. I kept thinking I could figure out a way to get up there. I had absolutely no idea how to make that happen. I was no astronaut in Houston or cosmonaut in Russia and, as far as I knew, you had to be one or the other to get into space. Still, I reserved a corner of my mind for the childhood dream of going up to explore amongst the stars.

Hamid, Amir, and I were a good team. Hamid was the money man, concentrating on bringing in customers and revenue, Amir came up with great ideas and kept our spirits high, and I was the CEO who kept everything together. We knew we needed to build an even stronger stable of engineers, so George Cowgill was one of the first we hired. I had met George when I was a consultant at MCI, and his soft demeanor, sense of humor, and willingness to help newcomers made us good friends from the start. He often asked me about our business and provided good advice, pointing out opportunities whenever he could. Even though it was a risky proposition to leave his safe and comfortable position at MCI to join a start-up, George put his faith in our hands and decided to join us. *Genius* is the word that immediately comes to mind when I think about him. Although he doesn't have a fancy college degree from a big-name university, George is one of the best engineers I know.

I had an open-door policy for all my employees and always encouraged them to be innovative and propose new ideas. So one day, George burst unannounced into my office, all excited about an idea. "Anousheh, you know the testing cycles at MCI and other companies are inefficient and time consuming. What if we design something that will automate testing? It would save companies millions of dollars and pay for itself in no time at all."

George went to my whiteboard and drew the details of his idea, then handed me a document containing diagrams and logic flows, saying, "All we need is off-the-shelf hardware and some good software engineers."

I've learned that the best way to make sure someone has thought through an idea is to try to shoot holes in it. Accordingly, I started asking

George all sorts of questions. For every question, he had a convincing answer, so I took the idea to Hamid. "We could automate the testing of telecom services using hardware and software that function like building blocks," I said, expanding on George's idea. "You set it up, leave it overnight, and get all the results in the morning."

Hamid was excited. "You and George pull together a team and get going. I'll see if I can sell the idea!"

True to his word, Hamid went to one of our clients and received a small down payment for development. This became the seed money we needed to field our very first product. We called it Fastest. Fast. Test. Get it? We hoped everybody would.

In 1995, the first customer for Fastest was our old friend, MCI, which recognized the time and effort it saved. Other companies soon lined up and we were no longer operating payroll to payroll. This motivated us to work even harder and to investigate other product ideas.

By then, Atousa had moved to Texas and was working with us. Baba Joon sold our house in Virginia and became a Texan as well. He had married an American woman named Debbie, and they both moved to an apartment nearby. With my father-in-law living so close, our time of microwave dinners was over. Every night, we sat down with him and Debbie and had a feast!

As tti expanded, we moved to a larger facility and added personnel to our software development team. We introduced three more products over time, including one of Amir's designs called Voice over IP (VoIP) Softswitch. It used the Internet to make telephone calls, and really took off.

Our company was now firing on all jets. We had about 200 employees, the best, most creative people we could find, and we had equipped two large labs with all the latest computers and test equipment. The consulting wing of tti also kept us in the know about the direction of the industry. We were perfectly positioned as an innovative, cutting-edge company that could deliver.

But I am proudest to say that tti was a happy place to work. We treated our employees like family. We never asked them to do anything we wouldn't do ourselves. If our people had to cancel their vacations to work, Hamid and I would cancel ours as well. We were the first in the office and the last to leave.

I also taught my employees to be self-sufficient problem solvers. As an example, we had a new employee who ordered a bookcase. The bookcase arrived and was placed in his office. After a few days, he asked one of his coworkers, "Who here installs these kind of things?" The reply was, "You do!" After seeing the look of surprise, our veteran employee continued, "And if you don't do it by the end of this week, Anousheh will come with her tool belt and do it for you!"

We paid competitively, had bonuses, and provided medical and dental plans, 401(k)s, and anything we could think of to help our people out. If I heard about any of them having problems—personal, financial, or in any other way—I would let them know we were there to help in any way we could. Loyalty is always a two-way street and it pays off.

We had fun, too. At one of our annual employee meetings, for example, my entire management team dressed in full *Star Wars* regalia. I was Queen Padmé Amidala and Hamid was Obi-Wan Kenobi. Amir was the young Luke Skywalker and George was Yoda. All the employees sat quietly in the large ballroom we had rented at a nearby hotel. All of a sudden, the lights dimmed, and in front of them on the large screen, the fantasy tti story began scrolling up against a background of stars accompanied by the movie's famous musical fanfare. It read: *A long long time ago, in a country far, far away, there was a group of strong Jedis from planet tti that were fighting the forces of the Lucent evil empire. . . .* (Lucent was one of our major competitors).

As the story finished on the screen, all seven of us, in full costume and character, entered the room from the back and walked to the stage. I was the last one and by then all the employees were standing and shouting and screaming excitedly. It was an amazing way to kick off that year. The space theme was always part of everything we did. Even the conference rooms were named after stars and planets and galaxies. It was my way of keeping in touch with my love for the stars and my still-burning passion to travel into space.

During all this time, I also worked on myself. When I entered the world of business, I underwent a transformation. I worked very hard learning how to give successful presentations and to stand up for my opinions in meetings. I had to be especially careful to keep from sliding into my comfort zone, which was to speak in a very low, unassuming voice. In a group of strong managers and engineers, I learned the hard way how important it is to speak up in a forceful yet calm manner. To stay ahead in a male-dominated field where a small, young woman might be overlooked, I had to be the most knowledgeable person in the room. Accomplishing that required hours of preparation before every meeting. I also learned to not let the opinions of others, no matter how robustly argued, cause me to make a bad decision. Leadership required me to be very discerning about what was best for my company.

I began to dress to make a positive impression. The way you dress affects the way people see you, and as much as I didn't like that, I learned it was just the way of the world. Still, as far as clothes are concerned, my final decision is always comfort. If it's not comfortable, I know I'm not going to wear it, no matter how good it looks. In my closet there are lots of black pants and jackets and what I call business clothes. On the other side, there are jeans, t-shirts, and casual stuff. There's nothing in the middle for me.

As for other aspects of my appearance, I've been wearing my hair long since I was a teenager. It's naturally curly and I do whatever it takes to make it low-maintenance. For the longest time, when we were working to get our company started, I even cut and colored my own hair. Sometimes I still do.

It saves me both time and money. My makeup is as simple as I can get it. I do only what is necessary and I'm on my way.

I also pay attention to my overall health. As CEO, I can't afford to be sick and miss work. When I'm stressed, I sometimes get out of control and eat everything in sight. My biggest weakness is chocolate. Because I am small boned, the pounds go on easily and are difficult to lose. Rice, which is a primary food group for an Iranian, is off-limits for me, as it goes straight to my waist. With this restriction, it's hard for me to enjoy Persian cuisine, but I manage. I would be happy if I could just eat fruit and chocolate. I believe in the benefits of daily exercise. I try to spend at least thirty to forty-five minutes exercising every day. It not only gives me energy, it makes me feel less guilty about my chocolate habit!

As our company grew, I had to work even harder to stay in touch with my family. Uncle Frank, the first person who told me I could be a success in America, still gave me advice. By then, he was pretty sick with lymphoma, but knowing that Aunt Chamsi and their son depended on him, he fought hard against that awful disease. Though he went through many rounds of chemotherapy, which caused him terrible discomfort, he never complained. If I learned one thing from my wonderful Uncle Frank, it was the importance of perseverance.

During this same time, my grandfather Buhbuh—who, with Maman, had moved to live with Papa in Los Angeles—also became ill. Whenever he had to go into the hospital, Atousa and I would leave everything behind and rush to nurse him day and night. This was the only time that I would take an extended leave from work and not feel guilty. Whenever I was with Buhbuh, I felt like a child in Iran again. I hugged and cradled him, cuddling while he read his newspaper. I loved him so much. He once wrote me a poem in Farsi. I cried as he read it to me. Here is my attempt to translate it:

> You're the sun that gives my soul energy, Anousheh.
>
> You're my daughter and there is no one else like you.
>
> As God is my witness, without you, I have no hope.
>
> You're my companion, my cure, Anousheh.
>
> As God is my witness, I have no one but you.
>
> You're the only one looking after my well-being, Anousheh.
>
> Come and give my body life again,
>
> Before I die, Anousheh.

Every time I put my head on his chest and heard his heart beating, I closed my eyes and prayed with all my heart, asking God to save and protect him for me, and to let him live without pain. God answered my prayers for a while, but then Buhbuh lost function in his kidneys and was put on dialysis. He was 91 years old at the time, and the doctors said he probably wouldn't last long. But they didn't know my Buhbuh. It was as if he knew I could not let him go. Unconditional love. That was what I learned from Buhbuh.

Whenever I was in Los Angeles, I went with him to his dialysis sessions. Sitting there, watching him so old and frail, my heart ached. As the machine sucked the blood out of his veins to clean it, it was as if my own life was being sucked from me. The first time I saw the process, I became lightheaded and had to fight back my tears. But I smiled and talked to him and played games with him to keep his mind off the procedure. One game we had loved to play since I was a little girl was called *mosha-ereh*, in which one person would recite a line from a Persian poem, and the next person would have to say a line that started with the same letter of the alphabet with which the previous poem had ended, and so on. My Buhbuh was old but his mind was still very sharp and he was positive about life. Even though the doctors gave him less than a year to live on dialysis, he lived for another four. The whole time I prayed for him. It was all I could do.

✧✧✧✧✧

As the 1990s cruised into the new century, tti prospered. Much to my surprise, I became something of a media star. As a successful businesswoman, I was profiled in *Forbes.* That was soon followed by *Working Woman,* where I ended up on the cover. I asked if I could bring Atousa to the *Working Woman* photo shoot in New York and they said no problem. We made a fun day out of it, feeling like celebrity sisters. *Working Woman* had a hair stylist and a makeup artist during the shoot, and not only did they make me look like a glamorous model, they also made up Atousa and let us have a photo session together. I keep the framed photographs of us in my bedroom.

Because I was now in the public eye, I was often asked to reveal my secret of success. Although I had never given it much thought, upon reflection, there were a few simple things that stood out: Sheer determination and perseverance, enhanced by having a great partner who was always there to listen, encourage, and help. Patience was also important. Apollo 13 Flight Director Gene Kranz famously said, "Failure is not an option." True enough on that mission, but entrepreneurs should expect lots of failures on their way to success. That's not all bad because failure teaches valuable lessons. What's most important is not to give up until the end goal is achieved!

Despite all the fame and prestige, there was still quite a bit of stress. With poor Uncle Frank and Buhbuh fighting for their lives, I was especially worried about Hamid's health. The truth was, we were both ready for a break. The boom in the technology market had resulted in many companies going public and monetizing their stock. Our employees had also heard about people in Silicon Valley making huge amounts of money from their stock options and they wanted the same opportunity. The bottom line was we needed to find a way to turn all our hard work into cash. We could either go public or sell. We decided to go public.

We hired Goldman Sachs to take us there and while we were preparing our paperwork for a public offering, a few companies expressed interest in buying us. One of the companies was Sonus Networks, a business familiar to Goldman Sachs, as they had taken Sonus public.

We told Goldman to let Sonus know we were amenable to their purchasing tti and negotiations began. These negotiations would prove eye-opening, and sometimes downright painful. For one thing, the people from Sonus were an insular boys' club. We'd be in a meeting with them and one would say he needed to go to the bathroom and, honestly, they would all get up and go together. Maybe they strategized in there, I don't know.

We knew the Sonus chairman was actually a shrewd businessman but we had a hard time with all his quirks. Our attorney would say something and the guy would turn to his people and ask, "What is he saying?" even though it was about the simplest thing. He drove us crazy.

In the midst of all this, Uncle Frank and Buhbuh both took a turn for the worse. I was torn between being at their bedsides and negotiating with Sonus. I would take short trips to Los Angeles and Washington to spend a little time with them but would end up on conference calls, pacing up and down hospital corridors. I hated myself for not being there for Uncle Frank and Buhbuh 100 percent, but I felt obligated and responsible to my employees. Their fate was in my hands, and I couldn't think of only myself and my family.

One thing became clear early on. Sonus wanted to keep Hamid and me in place until they were prepared to take over. We agreed to this only if we were able to have complete operational control, including hiring and firing, budget development, and so forth. I made sure all these promises were properly documented in the contract. Our negotiations, beginning just before Thanksgiving in 2000, kept going right through the holidays and into 2001. I came to hate the very sight of that contract.

Tragically, Uncle Frank passed away during this period, and then within a few months, my Buhbuh followed, all before the closing of the deal. In both cases, I was unable to make it to their bedside in time to say a proper good-bye. I held Uncle Frank's pale, lifeless hands in mine and, blinded by tears, kissed him on the cheek and promised I would make him proud and would always do my best to look after Aunt Chamsi.

I got the call about my Buhbuh's death as I landed in Los Angeles. Once again, I was too late. I was with Atousa and Hamid, and we held each other and wept. Hamid wrapped his arms around me and Atousa and tried to console us. When we finally made it to the hospital, we ran upstairs to Buhbuh's room. When we entered the room, Maman was sitting on a chair in a corner, wailing. Buhbuh was lying on his bed with the sun shining on his peaceful face. I put my head on his chest with the hope of hearing that familiar heartbeat one last time, but all I heard was the throbbing of my own pulse in my temple. I cried, "Buhbuh, I love you. I miss you!" But he was gone. Atousa and I held each other again and then went to Maman to console her.

The funerals of these two great men were a study in contrasts. Buhbuh's was a Muslim ceremony, while Uncle Frank received an American veteran's farewell salute. Although my heart was breaking during their send-offs, I could not help but think of all the ways in which these two men from such different cultures had molded me into the woman I had become.

With *tti sold* to Sonus, the financial news reports made it sound like we had stumbled upon a huge pot of gold. The truth was more complex, as the truth usually is. There was still a long way to go before the Ansari family could touch the end of the Sonus rainbow.

Even though we no longer owned tti, we tried very hard to keep the company employee-friendly. We hoped they understood how hard we had tried to protect them during the negotiations and worked to ensure they received fair money for their hard work. But as we discovered on September 11, 2001, sometimes it takes a tragedy to discover the way people actually feel about you.

I remember the day vividly. It was early morning and I was getting ready for work. As usual I was multitasking, my toothbrush in my mouth while I watched a financial show on TV. All of sudden, a reporter said there had been an accident involving a small plane that had hit the north tower of the World Trade Center. The screen showed dense gray smoke pouring from the building. Then another reporter said it wasn't a small plane at all, but a major airliner with lots of passengers. With the cameras focused on the towers, I watched a second aircraft fly into the south tower. This time, there was a huge explosion. My heart began to pound. I knew this was no ordinary accident. I thought it meant war was breaking out. But with whom?

By the time Hamid and I made it to the office, a third plane had hit the Pentagon. I didn't know what to do or say. Our employees walked around the office like zombies. We placed a few television sets in our conference room and people gathered there trying to figure out what was happening. As we watched, the twin towers collapsed and with them any hopes for the survival of the poor people trapped inside. All I could say was, "Oh my God! Oh my God!" Watching the buildings in flames brought back my recurring naightmare of the burning of the Rex Theater in Iran.

As the story took shape, it became apparent that this was a cowardly, unjustifiable terrorist attack. It also became clear that Islamic fundamentalists were responsible. In some places in the United States, a few uneducated people turned their anger toward anyone who had the slightest association with Islam or the Middle East. Even some Indian Sikhs were harassed because of their turbans and beards. I was concerned for my family. Who knew if we might be targeted, too?

The next morning, when we showed up to work, our employees and management team began to approach us individually to see if we were OK and if anyone had bothered us. The way they came to our side touched me in a very special way. I will never forget their kindness and genuine concern.

As the weeks and months passed after 9/11, the American economy staggered. The tech market, which had already been hit hard before this event with the bursting of the dot-com bubble, plummeted even further, and that was enough for Sonus to begin downsizing. Without consulting us, they also started slowly dismantling tti. Back and forth to Boston I went, fighting to save my people. It was a painful process, as Sonus kept cutting and cutting. Finally, in an attempt to stanch the bleeding, I told them that they were in breach of contract and we were leaving. Our bluff didn't work and Sonus let us go without a fight.

I cleaned out my desk and headed out of the building, only to be met in the lobby by nearly all of the tti employees. They applauded me and then presented me with a big corkboard with all their old tti employee badges pinned to it, along with a beautiful card. I was speechless and tears rolled down my face. I looked around and knew that, with the way things were going, most of them would be out of a job in a few months. I felt powerless and questioned whether we had done the right thing by selling. But then I recalled the rejoicing a year ago when we'd sold and our employees were able to go out and buy new cars, new homes, new motorcycles, everything they'd wanted. We had done all we could do. I had confidence in our people. They would land on their feet and with some money in their pockets.

On our way home, Hamid looked over at me and said, "Are you ready for an adventure?"

I wiped my red, puffy eyes and sniffed, "What kind?" I certainly wasn't ready for another start-up if that was what he had in mind!

But Hamid wasn't thinking like that at all. He said, "Let's go to Hawaii and figure out what we're going to do with the rest of our lives."

Now, Hawaii was the kind of adventure I could appreciate! We'd been on a long roller coaster, but the ride was over. It was time to go to a beautiful place, rediscover ourselves, and chart a new beginning.

So that's what we did.

A New Beginning

Our time in Hawaii was a tonic for our hearts, minds, and very souls. Like nomads, we moved from island to island, spending a month each in Oahu, Kauai, Big Island, and Maui. Amir and my Baba Joon came along. Atousa came over for a few weeks, as did Aunt Chamsi. There were no phone calls, faxes, urgent meetings, or desperate problems to be solved.

We stayed at hotels or rented houses. We drove everywhere, poking into little shops and finding remote beaches. When Hamid and I were alone, I sometimes pretended we were on a deserted island. It was like a second honeymoon. Of course, my husband could not bear to be cut off entirely from the outside world. He had a laptop and surfed the Web a little, shopped on eBay, and studied the latest health trends. Amir, ever the live wire, rented some jet skis and invited Hamid and me to try them. They were too noisy and fast for me, but the Ansari brothers loved them. They love anything fast.

Doing nothing was an amazing feeling. I would stake out a spot on a beach and pretend to read, but mostly I gazed out at the ocean and enjoyed its beauty. Sometimes I would doze off and dream of being back at work, running around in my usual business panic. When I woke and saw where I was, the relief was immense. Hamid and I began to look for property in the islands, but the prices struck us as outrageous. Although we could technically afford it, our mindset hadn't changed to match our bank account.

After a while, I began to think about what to do with the rest of my life. Even though I was happy living the island life for the moment, I knew it wouldn't be enough in the long run. I had a peculiar feeling that I was missing something important. After all, I was only thirty-five years old. Over the past few years, I had assisted a few non-profit organizations that helped children and women. This I vowed to continue. Yet, even though I was energized by this work, something else beckoned to me: my burning desire to go into space. *So, all right, Anousheh,* I said to myself, *you are an engineer and what do engineers do best? Solve problems! So get to work and solve this problem. What are you waiting for?*

Through Internet research, I soon realized that companies promising to fly people into space were mostly just fluff and moonbeams. No one was really building anything that could fly actual passengers. My research left me feeling depressed. When I told Amir about it, he searched himself but also came back empty-handed. We found it unbelievable that after so many years of astronauts and cosmonauts going into space, there was still no way for private citizens to go. Semi-seriously, Amir and I talked about building our own spaceship, even though we knew we were not rocket scientists and wouldn't even know where to start.

Our next stop on our travels was the Big Island of Hawaii. I suggested to Hamid that we should visit the Mauna Kea Observatory located there. Mindful of my dream and of our research into space flight, he said, "Maybe the stars will be your guide." I hoped he was right.

When most people think of Hawaii, they think only of the beaches. However, once there, you find huge mountains so high the air is nearly too thin to breathe at the summit. One of those mountains, Mauna Kea, is where the University of Hawaii, with the help of NASA, maintains an observatory. Hamid rented a sport utility vehicle for an exhilarating drive along the narrow, winding road, skirting huge gray lava fields. It was magnificent and stark, and I could almost imagine we were driving on the moon.

The Onizuka Center for International Astronomy is named for Hawaiian native Ellison Onizuka, one of the heroic astronauts who died in the 1986 *Challenger* disaster. When we stopped to catch our breath at the visitors' station, we met a park ranger who invited us to drive up to the Keck Observatory. I was as excited as a child who had received a free pass to Disneyland! We followed the ranger's truck up the rocky road to the peak. When we got there, I was surprised that it was much colder than the visitor center and the wind was howling. There was even snow on the ground. We had jackets and long pants but what we really needed were heavy parkas. Tears rolled down my cheeks from the cold and the wind but I was ecstatic to be above the clouds.

The ranger told us Mauna Kea is taller than Mount Everest by 10,000 feet if measured from its base, which is submerged beneath the sea. From its peak, the twin telescopes of the Keck Observatory could look across the universe. As the sun slowly sank into what appeared to be a sea of cotton, there was a magnificent burst of red and orange spikes, heralding the arrival of the first few twinkling stars.

We were allowed a quick tour of the observatory and then descended in darkness back to the visitor's station. There, we took advantage of a stargazing tour given by a graduate student. The night skies above Mauna Kea were magnificent. There were so many stars it was difficult to pick out the constellations. The grad student used a green laser that pierced through the dark night and reached the stars. He used it to outline the constellations and also point out some of the brighter planets. I told Hamid that I wanted one of those lasers for my birthday. Hamid made a mental note, probably thinking once more what a strange girl he had married.

Long after other visitors had fled the bitter cold and gone down the mountain, we remained, going from telescope to telescope. Though the freezing temperatures numbed my fingers and toes, I could not bring my-self to leave. I wanted to tell the stars to reach down and take me within their brilliant cores.

After a few hours, Hamid began to worry about my chronic sinus prob-lems and told me that if I agreed to leave, he would bring me back as often as I wanted and that we would spend every one of my birthdays here. I agreed, and with my face pressed against the window of the SUV trying to take in every last star, we drove down the steep mountain road of Mauna Kea. As we got closer to the main road, the stars faded in the orange haze of the street lights. My heart ached as if I had just said good-bye to old friends.

I stared ahead, deep in thought as we drove in silence back to the hotel. The next morning I woke, refreshed and happy, having made up my mind about something during the night. Hamid was already on the balcony watch-ing the ocean. I sneaked up behind him and hugged him and told him I wanted to go back to school. In fact, I wanted to go to the University of Hawaii and live as close as I could to the observatory. Laughing, Hamid turned around and lifted me up in his arms and said, "You're crazy, you know that!"

I laughed. "I know! But it's your fault you married a crazy girl!" I was so filled with enthusiasm, I couldn't stop talking. "Last night was amazing! I felt like it was really possible for me to go into space!"

"If you really want to go," Hamid said, "let's do something about it. What about those companies you found on the Internet?"

I explained I didn't think they were for real. They wanted most of the money up front and there was no guarantee they would ever build anything. I told him, "Look, until it's possible for me to go into space, I want to learn new things and know everything there is to know about the stars and the universe. By going back to school, I can do that. And you could go back to school, too—you always wanted to study psychology. We'll go back to school together!"

I wrapped my arms around his neck and kissed him on the cheek. Hamid said, "Well if that's what you want, let's look into it." I was so excited I jumped up for my laptop and started clicking through the University of Hawaii's Web site to find out about the programs, admissions requirements, classes, and so forth. We would have to wait until the fall to begin our studies, but it would give us time to go back to Texas and put things in order.

It was a great plan but great plans don't always turn out the way we hope. Instead, life was about to hand us a huge opportunity that would change everything, not only for Hamid and me, but for everyone in the world of spaceflight.

✺

We flew back to Texas, excited to be home. The office was overflowing with messages from people clamoring to tell us what to do with our money, how to protect and enhance it, what charities to donate it to, and so forth. My head was still buzzing from this onslaught when our secretary told us that a man from the X Prize Foundation had been persistently calling every week while we were gone. She said it had something to do with flying into space and added, "I know how much you love space, so I told him I would let you know."

My reply was instantaneous. "Call back and set up an appointment!"

A week later, two young men appeared at the appointed time. With a bundle of brochures in his arms, a nice-looking young man introduced himself as Dr. Peter Diamandis. His companion was a handsome ex-astronaut named Dr. Byron Lichtenberg. Hamid, Amir, and I escorted the pair into our conference room and then, while Peter set up the projector for his pitch, we peppered Byron with questions about his flights into space. I finally turned to Peter and asked how he knew about us. "I was reading your interview in *Fortune* magazine," he said, "and you said you wanted to go on a flight into space. Because of that, I was certain you'd want to know about the X Prize."

I looked at Amir and his eyes sparkled but Hamid raised a skeptical eyebrow. So many people had showed up with ideas about how to spend our money that his first reaction was always negative. With Peter, however, I felt immediately comfortable. He began to tell us about the X Prize Foundation and its vision of changing the paradigm of personal spaceflight. "The X Prize," he said, "is modeled after the Orteig Prize, which Charles Lindbergh won in 1927."

"Aside from you and Byron, who's in this foundation?" Hamid asked bluntly.

Peter told us the X Prize Foundation included an impressive group of trustees and advisers, including Charles Lindbergh's grandson Erik; Bob Weiss, a reputable and well-known Hollywood producer; and even the famous science-fiction writer Arthur C. Clarke. Peter said there was also support from entrepreneurs in St. Louis who were interested in following the tradition established by the group that supported the *Spirit of St. Louis* flight.

Although Peter used a lot of words to describe it, the concept for the X Prize was as simple as it was revolutionary. It was meant to encourage the construction of a spacecraft to fly private passengers into space.

"Into orbit?" I asked.

"No, sub-orbital," he answered. "But it's a place to start."

"What are the requirements?" Hamid asked.

Peter told us the competitors for the prize had to be non-government organizations and they had to launch a reusable passenger-carrying spacecraft into space twice within two weeks. "Space" was defined as 100 kilometers, or about 60 miles.

"What do the winners get?" I asked.

"We're proposing a prize of ten million dollars," Peter answered.

Hamid whistled. "Nice."

"We have a bit of a problem with the money for the prize," Peter confessed. "That's where we were hoping you might help. We have secured what is called hole-in-one insurance for the prize money, but we don't have enough funds to make the payments. The first is due in two weeks."

Hole-in-one insurance was a policy that insurance companies paid if an unlikely event occurred such as a one-stroke golf shot into the hole, or a private ship carrying humans into space. Typically, it was expensive. Hamid and I had been trading glances throughout the presentation. Both of us instinctively liked Peter and Byron. Silently we had already decided we would get involved. But to what extent?

We thanked our guests, traded some pleasantries, promised to give it all some thought and then ushered them out of our office. I couldn't stop smiling.

"Let's just let it sink in for a day or two," Hamid cautioned. "If it still seems good, we'll talk."

For that, Hamid got a big hug and a kiss. A few days later, with the help of Amir's persuasion, Hamid agreed. We called Peter and Hamid said, "We'd like to be part of this. So what is the next step?"

Peter told us title sponsorship was available at a cost of five million dollars. For that, we'd get our name and logo on all the advertising, press releases, and so forth. Hamid replied that we didn't have a corporate entity to take advantage of the sponsorship but, to get the prize going, we would put up the money for the insurance. We also had no objection if the X Prize Foundation sold the title sponsorship to a company that wanted the publicity.

"That's a generous offer," Peter gushed. "And, of course, we'll take it!"

There was a quid pro quo. I said, "We want the right to purchase two of the first tickets after the spacecraft goes commercial."

"Not a problem," Peter replied. And, just like that, the Ansaris were in the space business.

⁂

Over the years that followed, 26 serious competitors signed up for the prize, among them the Texas-based Armadillo Aerospace Company, Scaled Composites in California, the Canadian Arrow group of Montreal, and an Argentine team started by a young researcher named Pablo de León. "The one you want to keep your eye on," Peter told us from the beginning, "is Scaled Composites. It's headed up by Burt Rutan, who has a history of doing the impossible."

I had heard a little about Rutan already. I knew he'd designed and built the *Voyager,* which was the first aircraft to fly around the world without refueling. His company had also built the *Global Flyer,* in which billionaire Steve Fossett had soloed around the earth. Peter said, "If anybody can do this, Burt can. But who knows? Ultimately, it will be all about the best engineering and who can raise enough money."

We put our move to Hawaii on the back burner while I concentrated on the X Prize. Accompanied by Peter, I visited some of the competing teams. Although they were all confident in their designs, not many of them had actually built anything yet. More often than not, we were ushered into a small, shabby office and shown a PowerPoint presentation. That was it. No fabrication facility, no engineers at their computers, no machinists cutting metal, just fluff and moonbeams like the Internet sites I had visited back in Hawaii. In fact, I recognized some of the presenters as the creators of those sites. I didn't think they had much of a chance, given that it was the middle of 2002 and the prize expired in 2005.

In Argentina, we found the team of Pablo de León working out of a small, rusty hangar. De Leon's prototype of the *Gauchito* rocket was based on the *Little Joe* booster built by NASA back in the 1960s to test the *Apollo* capsule. Their rocket looked like a stovepipe with four huge fins welded to its bottom. On top was a mock-up of a conical capsule that was supposed to carry passengers to space, then detach and parachute back. It looked pretty crude. Still, I was impressed by the enthusiasm of the Argentineans.

Most of the teams were operating with very little money and making do with small donations and endless optimism. As a successful CEO who'd built a company from scratch with very little money, I was certainly familiar with these kinds of challenges, and there were many, from inadequate finances to untested designs to a lack of business experience. It occurred to me that if they had someone like Hamid raising money for them and someone like me running their show, they would have had a much higher chance of success. Of course, we weren't looking for jobs! Still, I also remembered how it was when we were building tti. There were a lot of people who were certain we would fail. Sometimes persistence and passion can make impossible things . . . well . . . *possible.*

We next visited Burt Rutan's Scaled Composites company in the Mojave Desert. Journeying into the huge Californian outback was like stepping onto a 1930s movie set. Scaled Composites consisted of a few big hangars fronting a long concrete airstrip. We were first led to a little cafeteria, its walls covered with pictures of Rutan and all his accomplishments. Clearly, he was the big local hero.

After we milled around for a while, looking at the pictures, a big man with crisp blue eyes and fluffy white sideburns appeared. It was Burt Rutan himself. He led us into the hangars where technicians were working on a variety of aircraft, then steered us into a conference room. Before beginning his presentation, he said everything he was about to tell us was confidential and he would appreciate it if we said nothing to the press or to the other competitors. He waited until most of us nodded our heads, then described how he was going to win the X Prize with a rocket plane. It would first be carried aloft by an aircraft and from there fly to the fringes of space. On the way down, a wing, much like a shuttlecock, would swivel into place and allow the craft to glide safely back home.

During the presentation, I studied Rutan more than the pictures and words on the screen. I sensed this was as much a personal mission for him as it was about winning the prize. He was obviously a strong-willed person and he even came across as a bit arrogant. His words and demeanor also told me he was wary of outsiders. It was as if he was really saying, *Leave me alone, let me do what I'm going to do, then I'll get back to you.* When I asked him a question, he just glanced at me, gave a curt answer and went on to someone else. It was clear he didn't take me seriously. This was no real surprise. After all, I'm used to being underestimated. I'm not very big, physically, and I'm also a woman. But, when all is said and done, I have a track record of success. I let Rutan be, figuring my day would come. And it did.

After my visits with the X Prize competitors there was little for me to do except wait, so I went back to my original plan of taking astronomy courses. I enrolled in an astronomy program at the University of Texas at Austin (UTA), which required me to commute more than 200 miles each way. I found a cozy loft near campus and felt like a schoolgirl again. I realized that maybe my first time as a college student had gone by too fast for me to truly enjoy it. This time was different. I was there to learn, but also took advantage of the perks of being in college. Not only did I have access to advanced computers and modern laboratories but, most importantly, a huge telescope! I registered for classes that were on Tuesdays and Thursdays, so I could drive home on Thursday after class and back to Austin on Monday. As an added bonus, my Iranian friend Elham, one of the Three Musketeers of Jeanne D'Arc, lived in Austin, where her husband was a part-time professor at UTA. It was good to have a friend nearby because I was always lonely without Hamid. Elham kept me company and very nicely listened to my blues. Sometimes Hamid would come to Austin so I wouldn't have to drive back and forth.

During this time, I thought a great deal about joining the astronaut corps in Houston, but an honest assessment ruled against putting in my application. I was in my mid-30s, and I knew my chances of getting accepted were slim. I also knew that most astronauts didn't fly for years and some never got a chance at all. Anyway, if a miracle occurred and I was picked by NASA, what would Hamid do? I knew he wanted to get back into the technology industry sooner or later and would need me to help. I began to wonder if my dream of going into space was selfish. After all, I had already been given so much.

Considering this, I counseled my inner self to accept my fate and just be happy. I was married to a handsome and kind husband, I had a wonderful family, a healthy body and mind, and all the possibilities in the universe. But no matter how much I tried to convince myself, I still had this constant passion to somehow get closer to the stars.

Then Hamid came to me with something new. There was a ship, he said, where we could buy an apartment and live aboard while it traversed all the seas of the earth. The ship was called *The World* and there were just a few apartments left.

"But Hamid, you get seasick," I pointed out.

"It doesn't matter," he replied. "Look, you won't be in space but you'll still be able to orbit the world. We can visit places that we would never see otherwise, and learn new cultures and languages. It's perfect, don't you see?"

Although I was intrigued, I knew I would have to give up my classes at UTA. We would also be far from our families, but I supposed we could always get on a plane and visit them. At least there was no need to worry about Atousa. She was back in Virginia, having married Kasra, a nice young Iranian entrepreneur and fellow electrical engineer.

I turned to the Internet to research *The World.* I learned she was the planet's largest private yacht, a floating community owned by her residents. I proposed a test voyage on a cruise ship. Hamid readily agreed and, as the fates willed it, we found ourselves in September 2002, aboard an Atlantic cruise ship directly in the path of Hurricane Gustav. Hamid took some motion-sickness pills and went to bed. For the next day and night, the winds and waves pounded us, but he slept through it all, waking only when the sea was calm and flat as a mountain lake.

"Did I miss anything?" he yawned.

I was grumpy. I hadn't left our cabin during the entire storm. My hair was tangled and my eyes were bloodshot. "Well, we're still alive," I growled.

Hamid squinted at the sunlight coming through the porthole, then laughed and reached for me. "So, now," he said, stroking my snarled hair, "I went through a hurricane and proved I can survive. What about *The World?*"

"You have such a one-track mind!" I scolded.

"Good thing for you my one-track mind at the moment is focused on you!"

How is it possible to resist such a man?

Hamid started negotiating, and though it took over a year before we got exactly what we wanted, we were finally able to purchase a lovely two-bedroom apartment on *The World.* Whenever we were aboard, it was as if the sky and sea swept all of our worries away. When we were invited to dinner, our hosts asked us the usual questions of where we came from, where we lived, what we did for a living, and so forth. Hamid always got a kick out of telling people, in a cool, matter-of-fact tone, "We are building spaceships." His statement would always be followed by a long period of silence, and then someone would ask, "What do you mean by *spaceships?*" And then Hamid would turn it over to me and say, "Tell 'em, my dear. Tell 'em how we're going to change the world and send people into space!"

People listened with their mouths agape and with a hint of disbelief in their eyes when I told them about the X Prize. I'm sure they were thinking, "These guys have more money than sense!" But no matter what they believed, one thing was certain—they knew we were not like anyone else they had ever met!

At night, when we had guests, I invited them onto our balcony to point out the galaxies and constellations in the sky. By then, I was enrolled at Swinburne University, working online for my master's in astronomy. One night I blurted out, "I want to live up there!" and our visitors chuckled politely until Hamid assured them I was serious. I quickly added, "Of course, I would rather stay with Hamid, or better yet take him with me!"

We didn't stay on board *The World* all the time; just when we could get away. In early 2004, while back in Texas and studying *The World*'s itinerary, I saw the ship was going to India. I remembered then that one of our tti employees from there had told Hamid of an Indian family who spoke an ancient language called Tamil and could tell fortunes by reading messages written on preserved palm leaves. For some reason, even though he isn't at all superstitious, the story intrigued Hamid. For his next birthday, I wanted to have a nice surprise for him, so I decided to take him to have his leaves read.

On the Internet, I discovered that our employee was referring to Nadi astrology. The origin of the leaves used to tell fortunes goes back over 2,000 years ago. At that time, there were apparently some very powerful sages who wrote down fortunes on palm leaves. Over the centuries, a number of families specialized in preserving and interpreting the writings on these leaves. I asked one of *The World*'s Indian residents how to make my surprise come true. We put our heads together and soon had a plan.

On the second morning of our stay in the Indian port of Goa, I told Hamid and Amir, who was visiting, that we were going ashore for a special excursion. The two brothers didn't question me. I had that look on my face that said I was in charge.

Once ashore, we went directly to the airport and boarded a plane. On the flight, I remained mysterious about our final destination and purpose. We landed in the town of Chennai, where Abhai, the cousin of our shipmate who had helped orchestrate the surprise, waited to take us on a dusty journey of 75 kilometers. "Kanchipuram, yes?" his driver asked, giving the Ansari brothers the first hint of our destination. Along the way, they pestered me with questions.

"Are we going to the Taj Mahal?"

"No. That is a thousand miles away."

"Will we see tigers?"

"No. I don't think there are tigers where we're going."

"Will we go hiking?"

"Only if this car breaks down."

The driver chimed in with some information. Kanchipuram, he told us, is known as the City of a Thousand Temples and is one of the seven sacred cities of India. It is also famous for its handwoven silks and saris.

"Aha!" Amir said with a comical expression. "I have it. We're taking Anousheh shopping!"

"No, that isn't it," I replied, laughing. "Although maybe after we're finished, I wouldn't mind!"

As we got closer to our destination, the surrounding countryside didn't look like any place a tourist would care to visit. Children were playing half-naked in the dirt, while their very young mothers washed clothes by hand and prepared food. I was getting strange looks from Hamid and Amir, so I gave in and reminded them of the story told by our Indian engineer. Their eyes lit up.

Finally, the car stopped in front of a tumbledown mud brick building in a seedy part of town. We went inside where we were met by three men, their naked torsos painted with intricate designs. Only a wrap of white cloth covered them from the waist down. People walked in and out carrying offerings for the gods. The air inside the temple was thick with incense.

Abhai acted as our translator. After he told them why we were there, the men took our inked thumbprints on paper, told us to wait and disappeared into the next room. After about an hour, we were escorted into a tiny room dominated by a big metal desk. We sat there silently for another couple of hours. Skeptical, we were carefully inspecting the room to see if we were being recorded. We were careful not to reveal our names or any other personal information.

Finally, one of the half-naked men came in with a stack of old leaves between two wooden blocks. He was accompanied by a tall man who spoke English. We each had been assigned a number when we came in, and the man who spoke English summoned number two. That was Hamid. The man asked him if he wanted to go to a private room but Hamid said we were going to stay together.

The man explained the process. The man holding the leaves would read questions from the information on them, the tall man would translate, and Hamid should answer yes or no. His answers, it was explained, would help to find his personal leaf. Hamid said he understood and the man with the leaves started reciting something that sounded like a prayer while flipping through the stacks. The questions began: "Are you an only child?" "Was your father a fisherman?" And so forth. Every time Hamid would say no, the man would discard the stack and go to the next one. This went on for a long time, until Hamid started saying yes to one question after another. At this point, Amir and I started leaning forward.

Our jaws dropped when the man told Hamid the name of his father, mother, and my own name! He also said the name Ansari would become very famous, and went on to cover Hamid's past and then tell him about his future, good and bad. The good I liked to hear but the bad I wasn't happy about. It was hard to believe what they were saying had been written so many years ago!

It was my turn next. Another Nadi reader came in with a different stack of leaves. He started to ask me questions. At each answer, he looked for a leaf then reverently set it aside. Finally, he seemed prepared, and I was dumbfounded to hear him say my name, the names of my parents, and my sister's name. At no time had I revealed this information, even when I'd made the appointment. He next covered the events of my life, ending with a description of where I fit into the zodiac. "Now, shall I tell you your future?" he asked.

I nodded and listened as he said I was going to be separated from my husband for six months while living in a different country, but that I should not be alarmed; it was not a divorce. Since Hamid and I had only been separated for a few days since we'd been married, I had trouble believing it. Then the reader said that after our separation, Hamid and I would have two children, first a daughter and then a son, but to have them I would have to endure many medical procedures. "Also, dear woman, at some point in time, you will become very spiritual. You will travel all over the world and your picture will be everywhere and many, many people will be talking about you."

"Can I change my fate?" I nervously asked. I was very much concerned about the prediction of a prolonged separation from Hamid.

"Yes," he said, "if you say certain prayers." Then he looked at me and smiled. "But why would you want to change what God has planned?"

After he finished telling me when and how I would die, he said some prayers and took his stack of leaves and left the room. My head was still spinning. I looked at Hamid and Amir. They were in shock. "What could happen that would make you go away for so long?" Hamid wondered. "It would have to be something very important."

I shook my head, then thought to make light of the whole thing. "Maybe I will go into space!"

"You will," Amir replied, perhaps sealing my fate.

An Old Dream Comes Alive

$\mathcal{A}$ s we had predicted, Burt Rutan and his Scaled Composites engineers were ready to launch long before any of the other X Prize contestants. I heard from Peter Diamandis that Burt hoped to launch his *SpaceShipOne* into space on April 12, 2004, the forty-third anniversary of Russian cosmonaut Yuri Gagarin's trailblazing flight into orbit. Technical issues unfortunately delayed this attempt, which was not meant to win the X Prize but rather to grab the record for sending up the first astronaut in a privately funded ship. On June 21, 2004, the Rutan team reached this goal with pilot Mike Melville at the controls of *SpaceShipOne*, zipping to an altitude just over 100 kilometers, the internationally accepted threshold of space. Confident in his design, Burt immediately announced he would go after the X Prize (which required two flights inside of two weeks) in September, and, sure enough, our invitations to witness the first flight arrived in the mail. I put a big X on my appointment calendar and started counting down the days.

Hamid and I spent most of that summer at sea aboard *The World*. I invited Peter for a visit as we cruised past Cape Canaveral. He loved sailing with us and found the concept and community of the ship fascinating. He gave a presentation to the residents, telling them about the importance of space and introducing them to the X Prize Foundation. He compared our ship to his vision of the first space communities. I was pleased when some of our residents joined the foundation.

Since no company had stepped up for the title sponsorship of the X Prize, Amir, Hamid, and I decided to go ahead and announce that it would be known as the Ansari X Prize. As September approached, Burt Rutan was all over the media with his vow to win our prize. I wondered if he remembered who I was, that small woman with the questions he'd mostly ignored.

The day came when it was time to pack for our trip to California. I eagerly looked forward to seeing Scaled Composites succeed, but on the flight out to California, I became nervous. The first time *SpaceShipOne* had gone supersonic, a nearly disastrous malfunction occurred when the landing gear of the little spacecraft collapsed on the runway, sending it skidding into the dirt in a huge cloud of dust. The NASA space shuttle *Columbia* had also been destroyed earlier that year, with the loss of her entire crew.

I have always understood and accepted that going into space involves risk. Distressed as I was over *Columbia,* I knew those aboard believed in the importance of their endeavor for the future of the world. As Kalpana Chawala (known as K.C.), one of the brave astronauts aboard *Columbia,* said two days before her flight in a message to her alma mater, Punjab University:"The path from dreams to success does exist. May [we] have the vision to find it, the courage to get onto it, and the perseverance to follow it." I also felt strongly that what we were doing with the Ansari X Prize was following K.C.'s path. Yet my anxiety about the coming flight persisted. I knew enough engineering to understand that when designing for situations that aren't entirely understood or predictable, there are always unexpected glitches. *SpaceShipOne* was about to be flung higher and faster than it had ever gone. What if something went wrong? Was I on my way to the high desert of California to witness a spectacular flight into space, or to see the end of a dream? While Hamid dozed beside me and the aircraft boomed westward, all I could do was silently pray to God for the success of *Space-ShipOne.*

Amir, Atousa, Aunt Chamsi, and my mom traveled with us. After driving for hours, we checked into a small hotel in the desert with creaky floors and groaning plumbing. I didn't sleep a wink all night, and by morning, my excitement and anxiety had only increased.

Before dawn on a chilly morning, we made our way to a chartered bus. Prior to getting aboard, I looked around and saw no less than James Tiberius Kirk, captain of the Starship *Enterprise,* hero of multiple treks across the galaxies, savior (more than once) of the planet Earth, and my childhood hero. It was, of course, actually the actor William Shatner. The first thing I noticed about Mr. Shatner was he was wearing an Ansari X Prize baseball cap. I nudged Amir. "Look at Captain Kirk! Did you ever imagine he would one day wear something with our name on it?"

The good captain spotted us and we exchanged nods. "Good morning," he said, cheerfully. "Quite a great day, isn't it?"

It certainly was, and I suspect Mr. Shatner didn't realize his presence had already made it an especially great day for Hamid, Amir, and me. As we trundled along the narrow highway in the dark, I kept sneaking glances at him, thinking, *It's Captain Kirk, Captain Kirk, Captain Kirk!* I thought of that Iranian schoolgirl I'd once been. How she would have howled with delight to be so near the great Starfleet commander.

We got off the bus in front of a brightly lit hangar. Behind its doors the bullet-shaped *SpaceShipOne,* mounted beneath a spindly airplane called the *White Knight,* was quietly waiting to make history. A crowd was gathering, most people carrying their own lawn chairs, to watch the show. A glorious desert sunrise glimmered at the edge of the sky and the winds calmed.

The hangar doors opened, and *SpaceShipOne* and *White Knight* were rolled out. Burt Rutan stood in front of the combined aircraft, his gaze focused over our heads on the distant horizon. After we fell respectfully silent, he told us the rocket-powered *SpaceShipOne* would be carried to an altitude of 47,000 feet by the jet-powered *White Knight,* then dropped. Within seconds, the pilot would then start the rocket engine on SpaceShipOne and head for the high frontier. He swung open a hatch on the side of the ship and invited us to have a look at the cockpit and the two passenger seats. When I saw that sandbags were strapped in those seats, I was dumbfounded and thought to myself: *What a waste.*

I told Burt, "If you'll pull those sandbags out, I'll be happy to take their place." I very nearly said, *I'm paying for it and I have the right to go!* but stopped myself just in time.

My comment got Burt's attention. While he stared at me with a shocked expression, I kept after him. "I'll sign any kind of release you like," I insisted. "I'm ready. Take those sandbags out. Let me go!"

"I can't do that," Burt stammered. "The FAA would revoke my license! Someday, well . . . I mean, we'll all go!" Then he walked hurriedly away and back inside the hangar.

Peter Diamandis was standing next to me. Grinning, he shook his head and said, "I bet you really would climb in and go, but I guess we still need you down here for now."

Next, we were introduced to pilot Mike Melville. Standing there in his black jumpsuit, I thought he looked a bit nervous. His wife and children stood nearby and I could tell by their expressions that they were *very* worried. My heart went out to them. Hamid and I made no attempt to engage in conversation with Mike or his family. I could tell they didn't need any hassles at that moment. I forgot about the stupid sandbags and sent a prayer up to heaven for Mike and his loved ones. I tacked Burt Rutan onto my prayer, too. After all, he had created something that might make it possible for me to fly into space!

As VIPs, we were led to a special stand and given radios to hear the communications between Mike and ground control. After a short taxi, the *White Knight/SpaceShipOne* combo took off and quickly climbed into the brightening blue sky. Before long, it was only a dot nearly lost in the glare of the rising sun. Several chase planes, armed with video cameras, flew with it. Aboard one of them was Amir, who wanted to see the event as closely as possible.

After about an hour of airborne checks and tests, an announcer told us *SpaceShipOne* was ready. Everyone turned to huge Jumbotron television monitors as the spacecraft was dropped. Almost immediately, its rocket engine spouted orange flame and Mike pointed the nose straight up. The flight was on! My heart pounded. I turned my eyes to the sky and kept saying, "Go! Go! Go!" I couldn't make out the little spacecraft, but could see its white vapor trail. Then, a camera on *SpaceShipOne* started providing us a pilot's view of the flight. The blue sky got darker and darker as the ship continued to climb. For a few seconds, everything seemed perfect, but then there was a gasp from the crowd. Something had gone terribly wrong.

SpaceShipOne began to roll to the left, then to the right, and then began to spin like a top. Later I learned that a wind shear caused the first roll. When Mike corrected against it, he inadvertently caused a trim actuator to turn itself off. At the same time, a cover around the rocket nozzle overheated and collapsed, causing a huge, jarring *bang* to reverberate through the ship. It was enough to make any pilot bail out, but Mike stayed with it as *SpaceShipOne*, twisting like a corkscrew, kept going up and up. There was deathly silence as the crowd watched the scene unfold. I held my breath and clutched the radio. I didn't understand what was being said between the ground and the ship until I heard Mike's voice. He said, "I'm OK! It's OK! I can make it!" Only then did I exhale.

At 76 seconds, the rocket engine finished its burn but still the ship kept rising. The picture on the monitors showed an arc of blue with white swirls. It was the edge of the earth! I heard an announcement that space had been reached, and Mike's voice came over the loop to say everything was OK. I was screaming, jumping up and down, laughing and crying all at once. Peter and I hugged and he said, "We did it! Thank you!"

I replied, "No, Peter, thank *you!*"

As the ship came down, we waited, craning our necks until they ached, and then there it was, *SpaceShipOne,* gliding peacefully toward the runway. As if it was something he did every day, Mike put his spacecraft down precisely on the centerline of the runway and coasted to a stop.

Everything else that happened that day is a swirl of light, color, and sound. I remember climbing on a platform with Mike, Burt, Peter, and Amir to the applause of the assembly, but I don't remember much about the ceremony. To this day, I get teary-eyed watching the video of that wonderful day.

A week later, we traveled back to California to watch Scaled Composites meet the final requirements of the X Prize. This time, everything went off without a hitch with pilot Brian Brinnie at the controls. There was no doubt about it. Burt Rutan had done exactly what he'd set out to do. I was proud to have been a small part of his success.

After Brian's successful landing, Hamid, Amir, and I went through another ceremony on the Scaled Composites runway, gave some interviews, shook hands all around, and then it was over. We had kicked open the gates to personal space flight. After the prize was awarded, billionaire Richard Branson announced that his company, Virgin Galactic, was going to team up with Scaled Composites to manufacture a truly passenger-capable suborbital ship.

It would, however, be years before it was ready. On the flight home, I felt uneasy and a little depressed. After everything we had done, my chance to go into space was still a long way off.

⁂

Over the next year, Hamid and I sailed the seas aboard *The World*. We also began to develop Prodea, a business dedicated to building technological wonders that would transform the world. I also was very involved with Ashoka, an international children's advocacy organization, and the X Prize Foundation. Life was good. What more could I possibly want?

Just one thing; I continued to dream of going into space.

When Peter Diamandis called and mentioned that the first anniversary of the Ansari X Prize flight was approaching, we discussed how best to celebrate. We decided to hold a space summit aboard *The World*. The idea was to invite the who's who of the space-exploration universe not only to celebrate the triumph of *SpaceShipOne*, but also to have a serious discussion on the future of private space exploration. It turned out to be a great party. Buzz Aldrin, who walked the moon with Neil Armstrong, came as our keynote speaker, and we had other speakers from all over the world, including Russia and Japan. To my delight, Burt Rutan attended, too.

The conference ended with a big party, during which Burt and his wife Tanya joined Hamid and me on our balcony under the stars. Everything was so relaxed that even Burt seemed to have lost his intensity for the moment. He joked with me when I reminded him of my passionate response to the sandbags in the passenger seats of his rocket ship. "I almost buckled you in," he said.

"Why didn't you?" I replied. "I wanted to go. I was *ready* to go!"

He looked nearly as shocked as he had that day in the desert.

We went back inside to hear Eric Anderson speak. Eric headed up a company called Space Adventures, which had contracted with the Russians to send two private citizens, Dennis Tito (in 2001) and Mark Shuttleworth (in 2002), on flights to the International Space Station.

Eric was also one the trustees of the X Prize Foundation. I recalled hearing about Space Adventures when I saw Dennis Tito being interviewed before his trip to space. It was in early 2000, while Hamid and I were still owners of tti. When I saw Dennis on TV, I told myself that if nothing else worked, I would do everything in my power to make tti so successful that I could afford the exorbitant price of a ticket to the space station. Now, here was Eric reminding me of that promise.

After his talk, Eric joined a group of us sitting outside and chatting. After we talked about the weather and the ocean and a number of other things, he leaned over and asked me if I would like to go to the cosmonaut training center known as Star City in Russia. "What would I do there?" I asked. He smiled and said, "You would train to go into space. Don't you want to go?"

Suddenly and unexpectedly, I was filled with misgivings. "Of course, I'd love to," I answered, "but Hamid and I have just started a new company. How could I get away?"

Eric responded with an invitation to at least come to Russia and look things over. He said his next client, a Japanese businessman, didn't have a backup, and I would be perfect for the slot. "I can arrange it if you like," he concluded. "What do you say?"

As the concept sunk in, I felt as if my brain was going to explode. If I went to Star City, I would be working side by side with people who had already been in space. "What's the next step?" I asked, a catch in my throat.

Eric explained that I would have to first undergo some rigorous and intrusive medical examinations. Then, if the results were acceptable to the

Russians, I would be allowed to enter cosmonaut training, which would last six months. "You realize," Eric said, "that I'm not saying you'll go into space. There are no slots for that right now, and I don't know if any more will open up anytime soon. You'll just do the training, and that's all."

Hamid sat next to me, silently listening. When I turned to him, he looked at me and I could almost read it in his eyes: *What are you waiting for? Here's your chance!*

For the rest of the evening, I think I floated about a foot off the deck. This was as close to my dream as I had ever gotten. But when Hamid and I talked about it that night in bed, I turned reticent. "Six months," I said. "That's a long time to be away."

"The leaves predicted it," he said.

Startled, I raised up on one elbow. "They did, didn't they?"

Hamid smiled at me gently and said, "Look, it doesn't even matter about the leaves. If you really want to go into space, you can't say no to this chance."

As usual, Hamid was right. If I got through the training, then maybe a slot would open up and I would be able to go. "But what about Prodea?" I worried. "We're just getting started."

"We'll manage. Anyway, I'll keep your seat warm. *Go.*"

I made up my mind at that moment. I was going to Star City, where Yuri Gagarin, the first man in space, had trained. The very thought of it thrilled me.

I got out of bed and went to the balcony to look at the beautiful clear night and tell my beloved stars that I was coming. I'm not sure how long I stayed outside, inhaling the clean ocean air and imagining myself in space. When I came back to bed, I trembled with excitement. Hamid held me in his arms and I put my head on his chest, listening to his comforting heartbeat.

How was it possible to live apart from my beloved for six whole months? How would I survive without him? He was my rock, my source of strength.

As if he could hear my thoughts, Hamid said, "I told you not to worry. Everything will be fine. That is my promise to you."

Knowing that it always helped me to sleep, he ran his fingers through my hair. Soon, my trembling eased. I curled up in my dear husband's arms, feeling all the pieces of my life, from my Iranian childhood to the glory days of Texas, coming together to allow me to meet my destiny head-on.

Third Stage
A Woman of the Stars

Star City

Hamid researched Russian medicine for weeks and concluded it was not as reliable as what we were used to in the United States. He kept after Space Adventures for a comprehensive list of the required exams so arrangements could be made for the more invasive procedures such as endoscopies and mammograms to be done in an American medical facility. Space Adventures provided the list but advised us the Russians were not likely to accept the results of private tests. Hamid tried to argue but the company representatives told him it was out of their hands, that the Russians did things their own way. Just in case, I went ahead and had the tests performed in Dallas and Houston and sent along the results, hoping they would be accepted.

In February 2006, Hamid and I flew from Dallas to Moscow. Our arrival was a jet-lagged blur. At the hotel, I climbed into bed beside Hamid and instantly fell into a deep sleep. Hours later, I was awakened by the insistent ringing of the hotel telephone. Hamid answered, mumbled something, and then shook me awake. "We've overslept," he announced. "They're waiting for us downstairs."

Panicked, I jumped out of bed. "But we put in a wake-up call!" I complained, hurrying into the bathroom to take a quick, cold shower. We rushed downstairs to the hotel lobby where two representatives from Space Adventures were waiting calmly. One of them was a young Asian American woman named Akane; the other was a tall, swarthy man.

"I'm so sorry!" I said. "We requested a wake-up call as soon as we checked in."

Akane looked puzzled. "This is Russia. Surely you know you can't depend on the hotel staff for anything."

She introduced her companion as Marsel and ticked off his accomplishments. After being employed as both a parachute and scuba diving instructor for the cosmonauts, Marsel had taken up photography and become an official photographer for the Russian Federal Space Agency. Now, he was the director of operations for Space Adventures in Russia. Akane concluded her introduction by saying Marsel knew everybody in Star City and could make things there much easier for me.

Marsel gave me a smile and a little bow. He was slim, had straight black hair, and an olive complexion. On the drive out to Star City, he assured me he was sensitive to the fact that I was a Muslim woman because he was Muslim himself from Uzbekistan. Per my request, he had asked for only female doctors and nurses for all my examinations. He didn't know if the Russians had approved, but at least he'd asked.

It was a normal day for Moscow in February—dreary and cold. The streets were covered with black ice and the traffic was terrible; everyone in a hurry, laying on their horns, cursing and shaking their fists. The flight over had made my sinuses raw and the Moscow air was making them worse. When I expressed worry about being late, Marsel replied in Russian-accented English, "Do not concern yourself. It is holiday in Star City because Anousheh is coming."

I hoped he wasn't making a joke. One of my concerns was the attitude of the Russians toward women in space. Our research had revealed that the few women cosmonauts who'd flown had complained about their treatment. The first woman cosmonaut aboard the old *Salyut* space station had even been handed an apron and told to get to work in the kitchen.

I reminded myself I had been in many situations during my life where being female made things more difficult. As an engineering student, I was a minority in my classes and, during our years with tti, every time I entered a meeting where Hamid was present, it was clear our visitors thought I was his secretary. When I introduced myself as the CEO, they were always astonished. It didn't matter. Within minutes, they realized I knew my stuff and was in control of the meeting. I had persevered before in the face of prejudice, and I was going to persevere now.

As we passed through the crumbling concrete gates of Star City, the official home of the cosmonauts, I fell silent, as I always do before a challenge. A group of men in dark, heavy overcoats awaited us outside a big, gray building. I would later learn this was the infamous Building Three, disliked by all cosmonauts because the medical exams given there could ground them, sometimes permanently.

Hamid and I were introduced to the officials but, in my excitement, I instantly forgot their complicated Russian names. Marsel led us to the second floor and down a hallway, permeated with the stinging smell of alcohol and soap. Although the building was generally drab, someone had tried to make the place somewhat cheerful by hanging posters and calendars emblazoned with the photographs of Russian cosmonauts, American astronauts, the *Soyuz* spacecraft, and the International Space Station.

We were taken to a peach-colored room where we waited until a nurse, dressed in starched whites, stepped inside and ordered me to come along. I followed meekly as her shoes made officious squeaks on the worn linoleum floor. She took me to an office where I was met by a doctor and a translator, both female. It was explained that I would first receive an electrocardiogram at rest. I was asked to undress from the waist up and I looked around to see where I was supposed to go. I was used to the American way of exams where you are given a gown and some privacy to change. The doctor and nurse said nothing, just stood there watching me. Things were indeed different in Russia. Without comment, I stripped down.

After the test, I was led back to the waiting room where a table laden with bread, butter, cookies, and jam awaited me. Since I had fasted, I was told it was now OK for me to eat. A samovar of hot tea was also wheeled in on a cart. Seeing it brought back childhood memories of *sofrehs* in Mashhad. Marsel must have noticed the expression on my face and asked me what I was thinking. I told about the samovar at my maternal grandparents' house. He asked what we called a samovar in Iran, and I said, "Samovar!" We laughed and talked about other common words in Farsi and Russian like *eshkaf* (armoire), *bouran* (blizzard), *keshmesh* (raisin), and so forth.

Marsel reminded me that Russia's only space shuttle had been called *Bouran* (or *Buran* as it was spelled in most of the Western media). It had been launched only once in 1988, and then retired. When I asked why, Marsel shrugged and said, "Money. Only the Americans could afford to fly such a thing."

After enjoying tea and cookies, I was sent to my next test, a comprehensive physical exam. I entered another small room containing a bed, a desk, and three chairs. Three female doctors and five male doctors were waiting. I sat on a chair in the middle of the room, the doctors squeezing in around me. Through the translator, they asked questions about my medical history. The doctors made entries in their respective notebooks and then I was told once more to undress to my waist. When no one made a move to leave, I sighed and did as I was asked. I was very uncomfortable and tried to drape myself with my blouse held close to my chest. It was a juggling act as the doctors stood up and moved around me, asking me to raise my arms and breathe and do different things. I think I had at least three stethoscopes on me at any given time

I went next to another room for a check of my reflexes. This was a simple test, requiring me to follow the tip of a pen with my eyes and get my knees tapped with a rubber hammer. On I went to yet another room for an eye exam. In each room the equipment was very low-tech compared with American medical instruments. It reminded me of visiting a doctor back in Iran in the 1970s. After the vision test, I went to see the ear, nose, and throat doctor. The equipment he used was a bit scary: none of it was disposable and I prayed that it was sterilized.

"Everything good?" the doctor asked. "No pain?" I kept replying yes, even when he screwed a big, cone-shaped device inside my nose to look at my sinuses. I was concerned about this exam because I had heard the Russians were quick to reject anyone with sinus problems, and I had terrible sinuses. In fact, the slightest dust or cold weather affected them. I had prescriptions from my doctor in Texas but the pills hadn't helped much in Russia.

The doctor stretched my nose until I thought it would tear off, and said, with great heaviness, "Your sinuses are inflamed." I quickly replied that I wasn't used to the cold Russian weather. He looked thoughtful, then shrugged and advised me to be careful not to get sick. I nodded in abject obedience.

For the last test of the day, I was instructed to breathe into a tube that measured the strength of my inhalation and exhalation. The doctor seemed pleased. "You are done now," he said and pointed toward the door.

I hurried out but was intercepted by a nurse and taken to yet another room, where I was fitted with a heart monitor that I had to leave on overnight. I finally returned to the room where Hamid, Marsel, and Akane waited anxiously. When asked how I'd done, I could only tell them I thought it had gone well.

On the way back to the hotel, Hamid told me that while I was being examined, the Japanese entrepreneur, Daisuke "Dice-K" Enomoto, had popped in. He was the next Space Adventures participant scheduled to fly and had answered some questions about the training program and the facilities. Hamid said he was very nice and had mentioned it was a good idea to look at the apartments in Star City, warning they weren't very luxurious.

"I don't need luxury," I replied, "but I do need clean and no bugs."

"I'll set up a visit," Marsel promised, then asked, "Are you ready for the rotation chair test tomorrow?"

"What's that?"

"It's a spinning chair."

"Which is fun," Akane quickly added.

I asked, "How much fun?"

Marsel shrugged and answered, "That depends on how much fun you think it is to throw up."

<hr/>

The next day we drove to the Institute of Biomedical Problems, also known as the IBMP. I hadn't slept very well, mainly because I kept worrying about throwing up in the dreaded spinning chair, which I imagined as a kind of medieval torture device. The only thing going for me was a little white pill I secretly carried in my pocket. The previous night, Marsel had drawn me aside to tell me he was going to bring me a pill. "It will keep you from getting sick," he explained. "Before the spinning chair test, there will be a break. Take it but don't let the doctors see you do it."

I didn't argue with him. It was unworthy of me to cheat, I know, but I was feeling quite outnumbered by all these Russians in their white lab coats poking and prodding at me like little boys with sticks. I decided I was going to take any advantage I could get.

The IBMP was small and shabby, and I could tell the old building made Hamid nervous. We climbed the stairs to the second floor and entered a hall so narrow that two people had to turn sideways to get past. A doctor I recognized from the day before greeted us and led the way to a tiny waiting room. Another doctor I recognized, a woman, entered the room and told us I would have three tests: one an auditory exam, another to test my vision, and then the spinning chair. The doctor removed the monitor I'd worn overnight and strapped a blood pressure cuff on my arm. When she commented that my pulse and blood pressure were both elevated, I responded, "Oh, I'm just excited."

The doctor next laid out a tray of small horseshoe-shaped steel implements with long handles. Before I could guess what they were for, she smacked one on the corner of my chair. When it hummed, I realized it was a tuning fork. She moved it around my head, asking me where I thought the sound was coming from. Mostly, it sounded like it was coming from everywhere but I gave it my best guess. She did this with several more forks, then put them aside and directed me into a booth and told me to put on a big headphone and to pick up two push-button devices and hold one in each hand. She said I was to push the buttons on the left or on the right, depending on which side I thought sound was coming from. I began to hear beeps and dutifully pushed the buttons. This went on for so long I nearly fell asleep and may have missed a few of the beeps. Coming out of the booth, the doctor was scribbling furiously and I feared perhaps she thought I was a bit deaf.

It was time to go downstairs to the infamous spinning chair. The doctors and technicians in the room looked at me as if I was some kind of lab specimen, which in a way, I guess I was. When a doctor indicated I should climb into the chair, I felt a moment of panic. I hadn't taken Marsel's pill! Like a doomed convict, I sat down. A doctor took my blood pressure, clucked over the results, and then he and another doctor put alcohol-drenched dressings on my right ankle and right wrist, securing them with uncomfortable metal clamps. My blood pressure was taken again.

"It is much too high," the doctor scolded. "Relax. Women always do better on this test than men."

If his comments were meant to make me feel better, they didn't work. When my blood pressure was taken again, it was even higher. From somewhere deep inside me, I felt a sudden anger and silently lectured myself, *You can do this, Anousheh.*

I breathed deeply and told them I was ready for another blood pressure test. This time, it was low enough to let the test begin. "Here we go," someone said, and the chair started spinning. To distract myself, I did multiplication tables in my head. After the first round, the doctor measured my blood pressure again and was astonished to see that it had actually fallen to normal levels.

A doctor asked me how I felt. "Fine, *kharashow*," I replied, showing off my rudimentary Russian.

"Can you do more?"

I nodded eagerly. "*Da.* Yes. No problem!"

Ten rounds of spinning were done. During it all, my stomach was like a rock, despite the big bowl of oatmeal I'd eaten for breakfast. A doctor said something and the translator smiled. "He says you are the spinning chair gold-medal champion!"

I broke out in a huge, conquering grin, which grew wider when the doctor handed me a piece of chocolate as my prize. I gobbled it down, then looked up and saw Hamid. He looked a little pale. "I tried to videotape you," he said, "but watching you go round and round made me so dizzy the doctor made me sit down before I got sick."

We both laughed. If I hadn't been strapped into that chair, I would have leapt up and given my dear husband a huge, consoling hug. I felt energized and powerful. Where Hamid had always given me his strength, I was now more than willing to give him some of mine.

Akane came over with more good news. All but a few of my American medical test results had been accepted and I did not have to repeat them in Russia. We returned to the hotel where I exercised and took a nice long shower. I felt great and was eager for whatever came next.

The next morning, I awoke with a terrible headache. It felt as if someone was beating my head with a hammer. The Moscow smog, the stale hotel air, and the alcohol-soap vapors of the hospitals had swollen my sinuses shut. Gritting my teeth against the pain, I met Akane in the lobby to travel back to IBMP for an electroencephalograph (EEG), a test that measures brain waves. I hoped it wouldn't pick up the terrible throbbing in my skull.

At IBMP, I was greeted by a beautiful young female doctor who fitted me with a plastic mesh cap studded with electrodes. She promised the test wouldn't hurt, but the cap was so tight on my head, my face turned numb. I sat there, trying to ignore the discomfort, while responding to the doctor's commands to open and close my eyes or breathe deeply. The test took about 40 painful minutes. Next was an ultrasound of my neck and the blood vessels in my eyes. All I wanted to do was find a cool, dark room and go to sleep. Instead, everywhere I went the light seemed to be ever more glaring. It was like nails being driven into my eyes.

Next was the tilt table test. The idea behind it was to tilt the test subject at various angles causing fluid shifts in the body. This is something that happens in the micro-gravity of space where bodily fluids are initially forced into the upper body and skull by the body's powerful leg muscles, often causing discomfort. When I saw the slab of aluminum with straps to hold my arms and legs in place, I thought it looked like something right out of *Frankenstein*. I had taken a similar test in Houston and flunked it miserably because my blood pressure, oddly enough, had plummeted. Two women in lab coats beckoned and I reluctantly climbed aboard the thing and let myself be strapped down. Electrodes were applied to my head and over my heart. "Are you ready?" one of the women asked and before I could reply, the table was tilted up to an angle of 75 degrees. There I hung for 20 minutes before being lowered back to horizontal for 5 minutes, then up once more to 13 degrees for 5 minutes, followed by a minus 15 degree head-down position. Tilting the table required turning a crank. When the women had some difficulties, Hamid volunteered to help. Soon, he was entirely responsible for turning the handle while the women urged him on. He even received a gift of Russian candy for his efforts. I was glad he was enjoying himself, but at the end of the test, my head felt like it was about to explode.

After an ultrasound of my leg, I began to feel a little better and was happy to hear I was finished for the day. When we got to our car, my headache suddenly returned with a fury and I slumped against Hamid's shoulder while Akane looked on in alarm. "I'll be OK," I assured her with a wave of my hand. "I just have a little headache. I've had it all day."

I don't remember much more about the evening except for Hamid tenderly putting me to bed and turning out the lights. When I woke the next morning, the headache was still there. "I can call them and ask for a day off," Hamid said when I groaned and held my head.

"No, I have to go on," I replied and staggered to the bathroom.

Fortunately, the day was routine blood work, more ultrasounds, and an EKG test, none of which required me to move my head. Then came a psychiatric examination. The psychiatrist was an older gentleman with a bushy white beard. He opened by asking me to talk about my family and myself. He then asked why I wanted to go into space and I explained that it was a childhood dream and I had a fascination with the mysteries of the universe. The psychiatrist nodded as if he'd heard it all before, then began some left-brain/right-brain tests. He told me I was right-brained—meaning I was more logical than creative—which I hoped was good for a potential cosmonaut. He then asked me to write down the names of the people who had made me "me." My list started with Hamid, then other members of my family including my mom and dad, Atousa, Buhbuh, and Uncle Frank. I ended with Peter Diamandis. The psychiatrist looked my roster over, then advised me that I was missing someone very important. I thought about this and mentioned a couple of good teachers I'd had, and Gandhi and even Albert Einstein. When he kept shaking his head, I was at a loss.

"Well, there's God," I suggested.

The psychiatrist smiled. "No. One more person who is the most important of all."

I had no clue and confessed I didn't.

"*You,*" he said. "*You* would not be here if it wasn't for *you*. Do *you* not agree?"

Naturally, I nodded my agreement. Arguing with a Russian psychiatrist who could wash me out of the cosmonaut program seemed unwise. Besides, I thought he was right. He told me to write my name down in the proper place on the list. I put it in second place. I knew he wanted to see me put my name on top but I just couldn't do it. After all, I would not be the person I was without Hamid. I pushed the list back at him, he glanced at it, frowned, and then put it in a folder. *Uh oh,* I thought. *Had I flunked?*

After a few more tests, including one that required me to stand on one foot (to check my balance? I'm still not certain) and drawing simple things like a man, a house, and a tree, I was released without further comment. My headache had subsided during the psychological exam and I was looking forward to a quiet evening in our hotel room, but was advised there was to be yet another test, this one a stress test on a bicycle.

Sighing, I worked my way through the knot of doctors surrounding the stationary bike and climbed aboard. The doctors soon called a halt to my efforts, saying my heart rate had reached 167, too high to safely continue. Every one of them began writing furiously on their clipboards. Desperate, I tried to explain to them that my normal heart rate was between 80 and 90 but they didn't seem to be listening. They made their notes, attached another heart monitor to me, and sent me on my way.

I was disappointed in myself and exhausted by the doctors and their demands. I climbed into bed with the clunky monitor strapped to my body. I awoke feeling sore and my headache throbbing. We headed to Moscow Central Hospital for an X-ray of my back. Afterwards, I was astonished when Marsel told me I was going to have to return to IBMP for yet another spinning-chair test. "Why?" I demanded. "I did so well. What else is there to do?" He merely shrugged in response.

Once more, I climbed into the spinning chair while the doctors peered at their little Iranian American lab rat. This time they told me to move my head slowly left and right while I was being spun. I did so, feeling queasy even as I worked math problems and sang songs in my head. Somehow, I got through without throwing up. Then the doctor in charge said something strange. Through an interpreter, he said I was like a rare mushroom in the jungle. Later I learned that mushrooms are very popular in Russia, so I'm fairly certain this was a compliment. In any case, I thanked everyone, bid them all a very good evening, and got out of there before they decided to spin me again.

The fourth day of tests required that I go inside a pressure chamber at Star City. Another solid wall of doctors, nurses, and technicians awaited me and I was told again to strip to the waist. This time they gave me some privacy and handed me an oversized terry cloth robe to wear. A nurse strapped a blood pressure cuff on my arm and stuck multiple sensors on my chest. I was told that I was going to the simulated altitude of 5,000 meters in the chamber. There were four chairs inside and I was told to sit on seat number three. I took this as a good sign because three is my favorite number.

To simulate altitude, air pressure must be reduced. It was explained that the pressure in the chamber would first be slowly decreased until I was at the desired altitude where I would stay until multiple measurements could be made. I was told to tap my feet on the floor to keep my blood flowing. There was nothing else I could do to help the results except try to stay as calm as possible. After I felt nothing unusual, I read a few articles in a newspaper that had been provided and, before I knew it, I was at altitude. After the technicians and doctors took their measurements, it was time to go back to ambient or normal pressure. They made it into a simulated rapid descent which caused intense pain in my inner ear. As I had been instructed to do, I yawned to equalize the pressure and, with some relief, felt my ears clear and the pain go away. After another round of measurements, I came out of the chamber. Hamid said he'd taken a lot of pictures. I hoped I hadn't looked too ridiculous sitting in a steel tank in a plastic chair with wires coming out of me while reading a newspaper.

Afterward, we went to visit the apartment where I would live if I was allowed to train. It was in what was called the Prophylactorium Building (Prophy for short), which was amusing to Hamid and me, but I don't suppose the Russians found it funny. My apartment was located on the third floor and overlooked NASA housing, which, in contrast to the shabby public-housing style of Prophy, looked like typical modern American townhouses.

Perhaps an explanation is required as to why there are NASA town-houses at Star City. Beginning with a series of space shuttle flights to the Russian space station *Mir*, the United States and Russia have been partners in developing space technology and building the International Space Station. Many American astronauts, scientists, and technicians are always at work in Star City, so NASA decided to provide its own housing for them.

Though my apartment had clearly been occupied by many others, it was reasonably clean. Still, I immediately tasked Space Adventures to see about some enhancements to the place, especially the bathroom, which had a broken showerhead and a barely flushable toilet. The word came back that as long as I paid for it, I could make any changes I wanted. I figured spending a little money to make the apartment into a nice place to relax was worth it. This definitely included a clean, working shower.

⚜

There was one big test to go. The centrifuge.

"What's the worst thing that can happen to her on the centrifuge?" Hamid asked Marsel.

"She could pass out," Marsel answered. "In fact, she probably will. They will attempt to stress her."

That night, Hamid and I walked to the Bolshoi Theater to see the ballet. It was a lovely show, but the walk in the cold night air was bad for my sinuses. I prayed my body would hold together for just one more day. I loaded up on decongestants, not even thinking what they would do to my heart rate. Consequently, I arrived in Star City the next morning with my heart beating like a scared little rabbit, and an exam revealed my pulse was much too high. I tried everything to lower it—meditation, calculations in my head, silently singing a happy little song—but nothing helped. An older lady came into the room and patted my hand and asked me why I was so nervous. "I'm not nervous," I told her. "I'm just excited."

One of the nurses held her hand under cold water and then pressed her fingers between my eyebrows. "What's that for?" I asked and a female doctor said it would slow my pulse and make me relaxed. I always had the feeling the women nurses and doctors were silently rooting for me. Finally, somehow, my pulse crept down to 110. Officially, it was still too high, but the older woman just shrugged and said, "Let her take the test." Although there was nothing said, I got the distinct impression these women wanted me to succeed. Most likely, they'd seen more than a little discrimination against females who were trying to be cosmonauts and helping me was their way of fighting back. After getting pulse monitors and probes attached all over my body, I headed for the centrifuge.

By then, my mouth was so dry from the decongestants that I could barely swallow. I was astonished when the centrifuge technician told me I was going all the way to eight Gs, which meant I would feel like I weighed eight times more than normal. To put it another way, I was about to be slung around until I felt like a small elephant was sitting on me! This amount of stress almost guaranteed I would pass out. I could feel my pulse rise again and I gave myself another stern internal lecture. If I was going to be a true cosmonaut, I needed to be brave. To demonstrate how I felt, I planted a big smile on my face as if I couldn't wait to be spun like a top!

My grin, however, didn't seem to please one of the doctors who was tall, thin, and had a morose expression on his face. While strapping me into the centrifuge seat, he admonished me, saying, "Look, this is a very serious, dangerous test. It is no joke."

My grin faded, replaced with a look of determination. The man I began to think of as Doctor Morose didn't seem particularly impressed. What did he want me to do? Burst into tears?

Then Hamid told me the centrifuge program director was there especially to see me. The director shook my hand and wished me luck, but I
wasn't sure he meant it. Later on, Hamid told me that Doctor Morose and
the director had told him they were certain I would pass out during the
eight-G test, which plenty of the professional cosmonauts did; but that he
shouldn't worry, not with the fine medical facilities Russia had to offer.
Hamid kept his opinion of that to himself.

Dice-K, the Japanese Space Adventures participant I was backing up,
was also there to watch me. I had a big audience! I suppose it's not every day
in Russia that a crazy Iranian American lady is swung around so hard she
faints. An old man completed strapping me in. As he did, he frowned and
asked, "Cosmonaut?" It sounded to me like he was saying, "You think you
can be a cosmonaut, but I don't think so."

Doctor Morose explained that any time I saw the little Christmas-light
LEDs in the capsule twinkle, I was to push the button on a joystick. On a
second joystick, I was to hold the button down continuously. That way, they'd
know if I was conscious or gone to la-la land. Lastly, I was supposed to look
at an eye chart and occasionally tell them the smallest letter I could see. He
also gave me some advice on how to handle the G loads by clenching my abdominal muscles.

They placed the chair in a horizontal position and pushed it up some
tracks until I was inside the capsule. The hatch slammed shut and there I
was, my heart racing. My earphones crackled and somebody asked if I was
ready. I said I was, and before I could take a breath, the centrifuge began to
move. Since there were no windows, I had no frame of reference. I concentrated on the lights on the front panel. Following Doctor Morose's advice, I
took deep abdominal breaths. The voice in my ear announced how many
times the force of gravity I was taking. At two Gs, twice normal gravity, I
began to feel the pressure on my chest. At three Gs, it felt like fingers were

pulling back the skin on my face. At four Gs, I was sweating. The LEDs twinkled and I pushed the correct button. I looked at the eye chart and reported I could still see it. The capsule slowed down and then stopped. Doctor Morose asked me how I was feeling and I said fine. I knew he was checking my vital signs. Four Gs had been easier than I thought, but eight Gs, twice the amount I had just endured . . . Could I take it?

After a five-minute break, I was asked if I was ready, and I said "Yes" with as much enthusiasm as I could muster. The capsule started again. At five Gs, my mouth was dry and I had a hard time breathing. When I reached six Gs, the pressure was enormous. It felt like my face was being torn off. At seven Gs, I tried to swallow, but my tongue was like a lump of wood. Lights twinkled and I pushed the button. *Eight Gs!* I was sweating profusely, my eyes watered, and I could only take short breaths. My chest was being crushed. My mouth felt as if it was full of sand. More lights and I pushed the button. I could still see all the letters on the eye chart except the smallest one.

I forced air in and out of my flattened lungs. I heard "Ten more seconds," and it was like I had just been given a reprieve. I started counting to myself, one thousand one, one thousand two . . . then I was back to seven Gs, then six, and then I could breathe again! Five Gs—everything was fine. Four Gs, and I felt completely normal. Then, the centrifuge stopped.

They opened the hatch and rolled me out. The old man came in to unhook me. I looked at him and said, "Cosmonaut!"

He smiled back and nodded. "*Da,* Cosmonaut!"

At least I'd won over one Russian. Doctor Morose pushed his way forward and asked me how I felt and what I could see. When I replied that I felt OK and could see fine, he finally seemed to relax. "Very good," he said, and pulled back to make copious notes on his chart.

Hamid was next to press in, saying everyone was amazed. Only a small number of professional cosmonauts had ever achieved the marks I had accomplished. I was proud, but not as proud as Hamid. He was like a little boy who was able to show off his wife to the neighborhood bullies.

When I got up, I felt dizzy and my knees nearly buckled. I was escorted to a changing room and allowed to lie down and drink some water. When I felt better, I changed into my civilian clothes and came out and hugged Hamid. I was flooded with a sense of peace and relief. Marsel told me he thought I'd passed all the tests but there was no way to know until I faced the doctors on a review panel. To my disappointment, he said that wouldn't happen for a few more weeks.

That night, I dragged myself through a celebratory dinner but my body had decided it had been through enough. I had a fever and my head ached terribly. My throat hurt, I was coughing, my nose was running, and I could barely breathe. I was completely and utterly miserable. Dense black clouds covered Moscow and obscured my beautiful stars.

Reflecting on the experience, I knew I had learned at least this much during my sojourn in Russia: pain is not defeat unless you let it win. After all, pain has forever been the woman's lot. And so I trudged on, determined to find my destiny among the stars.

Anousheh, age four, dressed to attend her first sofreh in her home town of Mashhad.

During happier times: (left to right) Buhbuh, Maman, Papa, Anousheh, Mom, in their home courtyard in Mashhad (Anousheh is about a year old)

The Three Musketeers and a friend in the schoolyard at Jeanne D'Arc: Soheila (left corner), Anousheh (next to her), Elham (right corner)

Elham and Anousheh with other classmates in school yard after the Islamic revolution. Note the long coats and hijabs (scarves) required even of school girls.

Anousheh and Hamid at Mauna Kea with the Keck twin observatories in the background. Here Anousheh renewed her love of the stars. Photo courtesy of Amir Ansari

Anousheh during Black Sea survival training. The water was cold and rough but Anousheh impressed her trainers with her tenacity. Photo courtesy of Space Adventures, Ltd.

Anousheh, Misha, and L. A at her surprise birthday breakfast. Photo Courtesy of Space Adventures, Ltd.

Anousheh's official crew picture. Photo courtesy of Andrey Shelepin/Star City

Official crew picture: Anousheh, Mikhail "Misha" Tyurin, Michael "L. A." Lopez-Alegria. Photo courtesy of Andrey Shelepin/Star City

(Above) Anousheh during her family visit before launch in Baikonur. First row (left to right): Fariba, Beeta, Aunt Chamsi, Mom, Papa, Atousa, Debbie, Kasra. Second row (right to left): Amir, Afshin, Hamid, Anousheh, Baba Joon, Jamshid, Tara. Anousheh is centered behind the glass. Photo courtesy of Space Adventures, Ltd.

(Left) Anousheh and Hamid in Red Square before her departure to Baikonur. Photo courtesy of Space Adventures, Ltd.

Anousheh inside Soyuz capsule just after docking to ISS. After so many years, she was finally able to make her dream of stars come true. Photo courtesy of Michael Lopez-Alegria

Anousheh during an interview with one of the major television networks. Note her coveralls with the American and Iranian flags. After much consternation over the Iranian colors, the number of complaints worldwide: zero. Photo courtesy of Pavel Vinogradov

Anousheh was surprised by Hamid's visit at the landing site. "You see? Didn't I tell you this was a love story?" Photo courtesy of Space Adventures, Ltd.

Training for the Stars

A NOTE FROM HOMER HICKAM

Perhaps a short explanation would be helpful at this point to explain the differences between the American and Russian government space agencies when it comes to private human spaceflight. The National Aeronautics and Space Administration, the American federal space agency, does not allow private citizens, no matter how much they are willing to pay, to ride one of its spacecraft into orbit. There have been three politicians who have gotten rides aboard NASA's space shuttle: Senator Jake Garn, Senator John Glenn, and Representative (now Senator) Bill Nelson. Garn and Nelson were key legislators overseeing NASA's budget and Glenn was famous for being America's first astronaut in orbit. There have also been a few very important people, such as a Saudi prince, allowed to join a space shuttle crew for a flight. In the programs NASA called Spacelab and Spacehab, active mostly in the 1980s and 1990s, scientists who were not in the federal astronaut corps were taken into space aboard the shuttle to work in special laboratories installed in the shuttle cargo bay. Although these scientists mostly performed very well, NASA has since used only its own astronauts to operate science experiments aboard the International Space Station. Interestingly, the Spacelab and Spacehab scientists were not called astronauts by NASA but were termed "payload specialists" and were not allowed to wear the coveted NASA astronaut golden pin, which is reserved exclusively for the federal employees in the astronaut office in Houston. Similarly, the old Soviet Union mostly flew its own cosmonauts (plus some passengers from other countries for propaganda purposes). After the collapse of the Soviet system, the Russians found themselves cash-poor with few goods to export. One thing they were good at, however, was flying people into space. Accordingly, they entered into an agreement with the American-based Space Adventures company (www.spaceadventures.com) to fly anyone who could afford it into space if they could pass a stiff training program. This helped keep the Russian space program afloat during some tough economic times. The United States, although a partner with the Russians on the International Space Station, also pays the Russian Federal Space Agency for the privilege of flying astronauts aboard the Soyuz to the ISS.

After a quick trip back to Dallas to wrap up some business, I returned to Moscow to find out if I could enter the cosmonaut training program. This time, I traveled without Hamid. Our new company was ramping up and there was just too much work for him to leave. I felt guilty that I wouldn't be there to help him.

On my first night back in Russia, Marsel and Sergei, the managing director of Space Adventures in Russia, came to my hotel and said they had made arrangements to see a Spanish flamenco dancing performance. It sounded fun, but all I really wanted was to unwind in my hotel. My bones creaked in the Russian chill and my sinuses were acting up again. Still, I went along and watched the dancer, my eyes glazing over as I wondered what would happen the next day. Would I be admitted into the cosmonaut program? With the results of my tests and exams already in, it was now out of my hands, and I worried excessively. Worrying is something we Iranians do exceptionally well. I think it's genetic.

The next morning, I chose to wear a black business suit. I wanted to appear as professional and poised as possible—a businesswoman of the world—even if I was told to pack up and go home. Akane, Sergei, and Marsel joined me for the ride to Star City. We went to a waiting room in Building Three where we sat with seven other cosmonaut candidates. It was a pleasure to see that one of them was a woman. When I entered, all the candidates nodded and I received a shy smile from the woman. We were all very nervous.

I had hoped to learn my fate quickly but it soon became apparent the process was going to be excruciatingly slow. One by one, the applicants were called to meet with the doctors. When my turn came, they went over every aspect of the examination results, delving into such minutiae I thought surely they had mistaken me for a fellow physician. In one room, I had to submit to yet another physical examination even though I had been promised they had all been done. Impatiently, I complied with the cold Russian stethoscopes pressed against my weary body.

After a break for lunch, we all returned to the waiting room. There, we were told we would meet individually with the program managers who would either approve or disapprove our candidacies. I braced myself each time a man appeared to call out a name, but all the others went ahead of me. None of them reappeared and I wondered what had happened. Had they passed or failed? I began to fear they hadn't come back because they had passed and I hadn't and they didn't want to rub my nose in it! When my name was finally called, I lifted my chin, smiled as bravely as I could, and walked into a big classroom. The doctors who'd tested me were seated in rows of chairs facing a long table, surrounded by grim men dressed in military uniforms. As I walked towards the table, I saw Shannan Moynihan, a NASA flight surgeon whom I'd briefly met. She smiled warmly and I responded in kind, although I'm certain my smile was a bit nervous and crooked.

Without any preliminaries, one of the men at the table congratulated me, saying I had passed all the tests and I would now be part of the Russian space program. While I tried to grasp this marvelous news and refrained from jumping up and screaming for joy, he went on to say that everyone would take care of me and that I should rely on them and trust them. He added a cautionary note, saying my high pulse rate was still of concern to the doctors. "You must concentrate very hard on your physical training," he scolded.

When he asked if I had any questions, I answered that I didn't have a question but I did have something to say. He frowned but nodded his approval. I thanked all the doctors, nurses, and technicians for their help during the testing phase, and then I thanked the Russian space agency managers for allowing me to join their program. I then stood, shook hands all around, nodded to the doctors, and left.

As I walked down the hall back to the waiting room, it all began to sink in. I was now officially a spaceflight participant! I couldn't wait to tell Hamid!

Within a week, I moved into Prophy, where I was pleased to find a new showerhead. The old toilet was still there but had been fixed. I enlisted Misha, the Space Adventures driver, to take me shopping. Misha didn't speak much English and my Russian was limited, but somehow we had become good friends. I learned later he was a retired race-car driver, which explained his skillful maneuvering through the crazy Moscow traffic. By the end of our shopping spree, I had a new mattress, new sheets, new pillows, new towels, and a shower curtain. I also bought several gallons of Clorox to disinfect the bathroom.

Back at my apartment, I put on rubber gloves and scrubbed the floors, walls, and everything else that could be cleaned. When I bought an electric kettle, I was entirely satisfied with my new home.

Every Friday, I received my schedule. It was printed in Russian and initially I spent hours using a dictionary to translate it. Because my translation was inexact, the schedule remained pretty much a mystery. After I mentioned it to him, Marsel began sending me a translated version. Problem solved!

After a few of weeks of initial training, I was allowed a short break to witness a rocket carrying cosmonauts into space. Hamid and Amir flew to join me and we traveled to the Russian launch facilities in Baikonur, Kazakhstan, where the *Expedition 13* crew was preparing to fly to the International Space Station. It was an unbelievable experience. As we watched the rocket surge skyward, I was laughing and crying at the same time. My heart actually ached from the excitement. The sheer magnitude and immensity of the launch just tore me up inside.

Seeing the launch gave me a renewed determination to succeed at all levels of my training. My classes included instruction on the *Soyuz*, the Russian space capsule, and the International Space Station (ISS), which was still in its construction phase but already quite large and complex. I also received eight hours of Russian language instruction each week, and two hours of daily physical training, usually a run or a bike ride in the woods surrounding Star City. Although I preferred walking, the Russians insisted that I run. The first few weeks, I had to push myself to keep up with my instructor but I slowly improved and began to love running, and especially being outdoors.

Living the city life had taken more away from me than I realized. For years, everything I had seen and touched was concrete and glass. I went from building to building, or straight from my home to my car. I had ignored nature. Living in Star City changed all that for me. I began to notice things like the scent of the pines as we ran along needle-strewn paths, and I delighted in small things, like bright green moss growing on a fallen tree. I enjoyed the warmth of the sun's rays on my face and admired the melting snow. I noticed the brilliance of new leaves and the bright blue of the sky. I enjoyed the birds chirping and the way the wind played with my hair.

I also spent hours walking around the lake outside of Prophy, watching it go from dead and frozen in the winter to alive with ducks gathered for a swim in the summer. I watched old Russian ladies with scarves on their heads sitting on a bench and gossiping while their grandchildren played. I even enjoyed how my face turned numb from the cold wind. I don't think I ever felt so alive. The only thing missing was Hamid. When I saw couples, hand in hand, I yearned for him so much, I felt like weeping. But I knew how much my husband wanted me to reach for my dreams. Love, I realized, causes pain; it causes joy; it causes *life.*

The rest of my physical training involved lifting weights and swimming. I confess, I've never liked to swim. When I first saw the cosmonaut training pool, I told myself there was no way I was going to get in that dirty water. When Anatoly, my coach, told me to go change into my swimsuit, I said I hadn't brought one. That excuse lasted a week. When he told me to go buy one, I returned with a swimsuit, swimming goggles, and a rubber cap. What I really wanted was a full diving suit with a helmet to protect me, but I didn't think Anatoly would appreciate that. After changing, I stood by the pool and tried to get up the nerve to jump in. I told myself, "All the cosmonauts swim here. What's the worst thing that can happen?" So I took a big breath, closed my eyes as tightly as I could, held my nose, and jumped in. The water was so cold, I nearly shot out of there like a rocket.

Gritting my teeth, I started swimming. After a few laps, Anatoly told me that I could come out and rest before going back in again. I got out and, without a word, sprinted to the showers where I stayed until I was sure Anatoly had gone home.

This became my swimming routine. I would close my eyes, jump into the freezing pool, swim until I was out of breath, climb out and run to the showers. But I soon discovered there was something even worse than the pool. After a couple of weeks of my fast in–fast out swimming routine, Anatoly stopped me before I could get away. "Anousheh, come to the sauna!" he demanded.

"No, it's OK. I'm good," I replied.

He wasn't having any excuses. "Anousheh, come over here," he ordered, and I could tell he wasn't kidding. The sauna, or *bania*, as the Russians call it, is a big deal for them. They spend entire days at elaborate sauna facilities where they feast and celebrate life. Understanding that this was a ritual, I obliged Anatoly's command by wrapping a towel over my suit and following him to the sauna. It was a small, steamy room with a half-dozen old men in tiny swimming shorts and odd-looking little cloth hats on their heads. They were all speaking in Russian and when I entered they stopped and stared at me like I was some kind of alien. I sat in the corner trying not to attract attention but I don't think I succeeded. I'm fairly certain I was the first woman in that sauna in years. In the days afterwards, I kept trying to dodge Anatoly and even stayed in the pool sometimes until he was gone, but a couple of times he caught me and made me go back to the sauna.

Despite the facilities where he coached, I really liked Anatoly. He worked hard to make me into a good cosmonaut and always gave me words of encouragement. I hoped he liked me, too, but I wonder what he really thought about me, this strange woman who hated the water and the steamy familiarity of a good Russian sauna.

✧⋆✧⋆✧

No matter how hard I tried during my classes, I had the feeling the Russian instructors weren't taking me seriously. For one thing, I wasn't a primary crew member, so there was no guarantee I would ever go into space. Why care about me if I was never going to fly? They probably viewed me as a silly, rich, spoiled American woman who was pretend-training just for fun. Nothing was ever said explicitly, but a shrug here, some rolled eyes there, and I got the message.

I have never been the type of student who jumps up to answer a teacher's question. I need time to let information sink in. I also tend to overanalyze, so obvious answers sometimes elude me. Because of these quirks, I suppose it was hard for the Russian instructors to assess whether I understood what they were telling me. But once I'd taken the training materials back to my room to study, I usually understood everything and did well on the tests. On my first official test of the systems in the Russian segment of the International Space Station (called the FGB), I went into the simulator and completed every procedure perfectly. I think the Russians were surprised, and it made me happy to prove to them what I could do.

Occasionally, an instructor would use an intimidation tactic. For instance, I once entered a classroom and there was a picture of a naked woman being projected on a screen. As I sat down, I noticed the instructor was intently watching to see my reaction. I glanced at the screen and then casually started talking to Dice-K who was seated beside me. I don't think Dice-K ever saw the picture at all. The smirk on the instructor's face disappeared and he went on to start the class. Now, I had a smirk on my face but I did my best to hide it.

✠

On *April 12, 2006,* I had a moment to reflect on the accomplishments of a true pioneer. As I was walking back from class, I saw a large gathering in front of the statue of Yuri Gagarin, the first human in space, which sits in the main square of Star City. At full attention before the statue was a row of men in blue uniforms—military cadets, I later learned—and behind them a knot of stern dignitaries in dark suits. Gathered less formally were many residents of Star City. I had come across a celebration of Cosmonaut Day, held annually all over Russia on the anniversary of Gagarin's spaceflight in 1961.

I happily joined in the celebration and saw Bill McArthur, the American astronaut. Bill had recently returned from a six-month mission on the space station. He didn't seem any worse for his experience, quite steady on his feet as far as I could tell, and was enjoying the spectacle. I hadn't met him, so I stayed on the periphery of the crowd, surreptitiously watching with great interest.

I was also pleased to see Valentina Tereshkova, the first woman in space. I had met her earlier at a celebration of the return of the ISS Expedition 12 crew. Marsel introduced us and explained I was training as a backup. Through Marsel, she told me I was going to fly very soon. I thanked her for her confidence in me.

The roar of a jet engine overhead caused me to look up as a MiG high-performance military aircraft, painted in the red, white, and blue colors of the Russian flag, flew overhead, twisted on its side, then shot straight up. At the top of its climb, it pitched over, swept down, and performed some acrobatic moves across the sky. The cadets marched forward with baskets of flowers and placed them at the foot of the statue. The officials and important guests followed with more flowers until Gagarin's image was festooned with a colorful display. The band struck up a lively tune and the cadets marched away. It was an impressive display and made me wish that the United States had a special day of ceremony for our astronauts. I am often astonished when talking to American students who have no idea who Yuri Gagarin was, or even Neil Armstrong. We must do a better job of educating our children.

Later that week, Brazilian astronaut Marcos Pontes, whom I had met and shared a few lunches with at the cosmonaut cafeteria prior to his flight, came to my apartment to give me a gift of some souvenir patches from his ten-day space station mission. He was still excited about going into space and said it had changed him as a person in the best possible way. Since I had attended his launch, I burned a CD of photos I had taken that night and sent it by messenger to his room. The next day, Marcos came to my apartment to give me a flattened silver coin, saying, "This is the coin that they put under the train when my *Soyuz* was delivered to the launch pad. It brought me back safely, and I'm giving it to you for your flight."

Overwhelmed by the gesture, I blurted, "But Marcos, I can't accept this! I may not fly for years!"

He smiled and said, "I have a feeling your time will come a lot sooner than you think."

After Marcos left, I closed the door and stood there for a few minutes. First Valentina Tereshkova and now Marcos Pontes had predicted I was going into space sooner than I thought. I caught myself contemplating how that might happen. Was there an empty seat I didn't know about? My deal with Space Adventures was only to train, then go home and wait for a seat to open up. I couldn't imagine why or how it might work out any other way.

The day came when I was to be fitted for a *Soyuz* seat liner. The liner is a specially made foam mold that cushions a cosmonaut during launch and reentry from space. The theory is that a custom fit will soften the extreme forces likely to be encountered, especially during the landing. The factory for the liner was on the other side of Moscow, so off I went with one of our translators. At the factory, there was a whole crew of people waiting for me. Nothing, it seems, can be done in Russia without an army.

The device used to make the casting was shaped like a large oval tub. Wearing a special set of long underwear, I got into the tub and lay on my back with my knees drawn up, the required position to sit in a *Soyuz*. Big sponges were tucked all around me so that I was immobilized. Two men, one with a flashing gold tooth, poured buckets of a thick, milky liquid all around me. Submerged in this goop, I reflected upon how willing I was to endure nearly anything for a chance to fly into space. After waiting about ten minutes for the mold to set, I was pulled out with a crane, sent to strip down, take a quick shower, and put on another set of long johns.

I once again climbed into the tub to have the procedure repeated for a mold of my lower body. After cleaning up again, I changed into yet another pair of long underwear for the final fitting, this one of my entire body. Feeling a bit like the princess in the "Princess and the Pea," who required dozens of mattresses to sleep because she was so sensitive, I commented on some small discomforts and the technicians sculpted around them. I called the leader, the man with the gold tooth, my Michelangelo.

Next came the best part of the whole exercise: putting on a spacesuit. I had never worn a spacesuit and was excited to try one on. The Russians have two types of spacesuits, each designed for different jobs. The spacesuit cosmonauts wear to go outside into space is known as the Orlon (or Sea Eagle). The suit they brought out for me was the type that is used only for launch and landing. This suit is known as the Sokol (which translates to Falcon in English).

The Sokol suit proved much heavier than I imagined, and also required a couple of technicians to help me get zipped up, but I enjoyed every second inside it. I was lowered into the liner with the helmet cover closed, as it would be during launch and landing. While the technicians continued to sculpt around me, I amused myself by pretending to actually be in space.

Next I had to learn how to put on the suit by myself, climb into a mockup seat of the *Soyuz* capsule, and perform a suit-leak check. The suit assigned to me was about two sizes too big and I felt lost inside it, like a rabbit peeking out of its hole. To test for leaks, I had to turn a valve and read a pressure gauge, and was soaking wet from perspiration by the time I finished. I gave the instructors a willing smile to indicate I was ready for anything else they wanted to send my way but this was met with frowns. I didn't seem to be getting anywhere in the respect department.

The next week, bright and early, I was taken to the facility where the *Soyuz* space capsules are assembled and tested. Dice-K was there and introduced me to cosmonaut Mikhail Tyurin, a small, powerfully built man with a thick moustache. He was the commander of Dice-K's upcoming flight. I shook his hand and he turned around to continue a serious conversation with some of the technicians.

The training of the day required us to examine and identify components of the actual capsule that was going to carry Dice-K, Tyurin, and American astronaut Michael Lopez-Alegria into space. Before entering the room that contained the capsule, we had to put on clean-room clothes consisting of coveralls, shoe covers, and caps. Then we climbed a scaffold and peered inside the *Soyuz* while the instructors went over the different aspects of its design. When Dice-K and I asked questions, it was Tyurin who answered, all the while reviewing the release notes from the engineers and checking the vehicle. This cosmonaut commander certainly knew his stuff. When he invited me to call him Misha, his nickname, I felt quite honored.

We each donned a Sokol suit and climbed into the capsule from an attached habitation compartment, which the Russians called the BO (short for the Russian *bytovoi otsek;* pronounced *beh-o*). Since his training was more important than mine, Dice-K was the first to try it. There wasn't enough room for me to watch from inside the BO, so I went into another room to observe a *Progress* supply capsule being lifted by a huge crane onto a railcar for transport to the launch facility in Baikonur.

The *Progress* is an interesting series of space vehicles. Modeled after the *Soyuz* and launched aboard the same kind of rocket, they are automated cargo craft that, every couple of months or so, carries more than two and a half tons of supplies to the International Space Station. Although it isn't a new design, first flown back in 1974, NASA has nothing like it. After the cargo is unloaded manually by the ISS crew, a *Progress* is filled with trash and wastewater, and sent hurtling into the atmosphere to burn up. Like most Russian space hardware, it is very reliable. The only time one of them caused any problems at all occurred during the resupply of the old *Mir* station. When a cosmonaut tried to manually coax a *Progress* in for a docking, he instead crashed it into the station, creating an air leak, which nearly meant that the *Mir* would have to be abandoned.

I enjoyed watching the shiny new *Progress* as it was loaded on its transport, but I also fretted the entire time. How would I do when I had to climb inside the *Soyuz,* encumbered by a heavy spacesuit? What if I messed up in front of Misha?

Finally, it was my turn. The Sokol suit assigned to me turned out to be one Misha had worn into space. Since he wasn't all that big, it was only slightly too large for me, but still very heavy. I climbed into the BO and gathered all my energy to lower myself from its inner hatch into the *Soyuz* capsule. This is a bit like performing a pull-up while wearing weights, but I clumsily managed the maneuver without making a fool out of myself. Of the three seats, the one designated for me was on the right. Once I had climbed into it, my job was to hook up all the suit connections. I remembered my training and began the process while Misha watched me from the middle seat. From the beginning, I had felt that the cosmonaut commanders disapproved of us so-called spaceflight participants, mainly because we were extra work and responsibility for them. With Misha's critical eyes on me, I felt the pressure.

Sweat trickled into my eyes as I worked hard to do everything perfectly. All went well until I tried to connect my seat harness and I couldn't find one of the belts. Misha reached over to help, but it wasn't easy in that cramped space. When I was finally hooked up, my seat was raised by remote control. This was, Misha said, the position during the final stages of a landing. I checked to make sure I could reach everything on the instrument panel, and then Misha said, "Now we have to get out." I summoned all my strength, unhooked everything from my suit, and exited. Misha climbed out behind me with ease.

Feeling somewhat pleased with myself, I went to the dressing room and changed. Not only had I managed to accomplish the day's tasks without embarrassment, I believed I had made a friend in Cosmonaut Commander Mikhail "Misha" Tyurin. I was more than a little jealous of Dice-K because Misha was his commander. I wondered, if and when I got to fly, who would be my commander? I only hoped he would be half as nice and knowledgeable as Misha.

After cleaning up, Dice-K and I entered a meeting room where Misha was waiting for us. With a friendly smile, he told us we had done well and that he was proud of us. One more milestone had been accomplished. I had no inkling that my next big hurdle would be pure survival, Russian-style.

In the first few months of training, almost all of my time was spent with Dice-K, which was the name he preferred, rather than Daisuke Enomoto. I learned that he was a Japanese entrepreneur who had helped found an extremely lucrative Internet start-up called Livedoor. When he'd sold it, Dice-K found himself with a fat bank account and a dream of going into space. Space Adventures was happy to help him out. My first impression of Dice-K was that he looked a bit fragile and pale. He always wore the same poker-faced expression and rarely smiled. He was obviously very intelligent, but I'd also heard he could be a bit eccentric. He was a rabid fan of the anime cartoon series *Gundam,* which featured humans wearing robot suits while fighting space monsters. One of our interpreters gleefully revealed to me that Dice-K planned on wearing the costume of one of the *Gundam* characters on board the space station. She wondered what the NASA astronauts would make of that!

I quite enjoyed my time with Dice-K. He was always pleasant and courteous. We took the same classes and simulations and encouraged one another as we went along. After a while, he started to train exclusively with the Expedition 14 crew, the American astronaut Michael Lopez-Alegria and my new friend cosmonaut Misha Tyurin. Because I wasn't designated for any mission, I felt a bit like an orphan until I was assigned to train with astronaut Peggy Whitson and cosmonaut Yuri Malenchenko, the backups for Expedition 14 and the main crew for Expedition 16. There was a Malaysian cosmonaut who was scheduled to fill the right seat of that mission, but I was allowed to substitute for him until he arrived in Star City.

I had an immediate affinity for Peggy. A biochemist from Iowa, she had already spent six months aboard the ISS during Expedition 5, and had even performed work outside the station in a Russian spacesuit. She was a woman of strong character and intelligence. When we started to train as a crew, she and I spent a lot of time together. I could tell she was sizing me up to determine whether I was there just for the ride or if I had a genuine interest in space. During simulations, she gave me small tasks to perform. Perhaps impressed when I did them without error, she began to explain everything to me in detail and, since her Russian was excellent, translated for me when necessary. In a way, she became my mentor. I like to imagine that had my life taken a different turn and I had become a professional astronaut, I would have been a lot like Peggy. Throughout the rest of my training program, I learned much from her, including little things like the best observation stations aboard the ISS, how to wash my hair and clean myself in space, and, of course, the use of the space toilet (everyone's favorite subject).

Getting to know Yuri Malenchenko, Peggy's crewmate, proved harder. Though his English was excellent, Yuri usually had little to say. He seemed to be a very serious man who worked slowly and meticulously, with little time to waste in idle conversation. While seated next to him in the simulator, I watched him go through a series of manual docking and undocking exercises. It was obvious that he knew how to drive the *Soyuz* with his eyes closed. I started calling him Cool Hand Luke.

As my training progressed, I got it into my head that I really wanted to fly with Peggy and Yuri and decided to push to make that happen. I asked Space Adventures to negotiate with the Russians to put me, rather than the Malaysian cosmonaut, on Expedition 16. Space Adventures said they would do what they could, but asked me to be patient because the odds were very much against me. As time went by in my training, I got more and more anxious. What if I never got assigned? What if I went through all this for nothing? I had more than a few sleepless nights worrying about such things.

In late May, I was separated from Peggy and Yuri and sent off with Dice-K to the town of Sevastopol in the country of Ukraine for water-landing survival training at an old Soviet naval base. We arrived in the afternoon and checked into the Hotel Krim. According to the interpreters, I had the best room in the hotel because it had its own water heater. All the other rooms only had hot water for one hour in the morning and one at night, and if you didn't happen to be in the hotel during those hours, you were out of luck.

On the first night in town Dice-K and I went to dinner at a local restaurant with Roman, our interpreter, and Dennis, our Space Adventures chaperone. While we were there, a few Russian training personnel came by and things began to get boisterous. We were asked to join in a round of drinks, and though I courteously declined, they soon had Dice-K drinking vodka until his face turned a bright cherry red and he began to look a bit ill. I tried to help Dice-K leave but the band started playing Russian music and everybody began dancing. The music and people were so loud, I was certain I was going to get a headache.

Then a Ukrainian woman stepped up to the microphone and sang what I recognized as a Persian dance song. I couldn't quite get over it. Here I was, training to be a cosmonaut, sitting in a café in Sevastopol, and listening to a familiar Iranian song! In all my wildest dreams, I could not have imagined such a moment. Dice-K and I finally got back to the hotel around midnight and I gratefully collapsed onto the lumpy bed, the Persian song still in my head.

We met for breakfast in the hotel dining room. I was fresh and excited about the plan for the day, but Dice-K looked like he'd been dragged through the streets. When I said good morning, he groaned. I presumed all the vodka he'd drunk the night before was still doing a number on him.

Eating in the Hotel Krim was an odd experience. At night, the restaurant became a disco and there was a mirror ball overhead. The walls and ceiling were strung with crepe paper and decorations and everything stunk of beer and vodka. The room was also being remodeled with bags of cement, plaster, and lumber stacked everywhere. The breakfast menu consisted of oatmeal, yogurt, and a meat dish. I stuck with oatmeal and yogurt; the former a sticky paste, the latter pretty good and sweet.

The others in the dining room included Yuri Gidzenko, the Expedition 1 *Soyuz* commander, and a few of my instructors from Star City. They were mostly silent and absorbed with their meals. I got the impression they were all survivors of a rough night of partying.

After breakfast, we walked to the harbor and boarded a small boat. The weather had turned cloudy, gray, and drizzly, and Roman said there was a chance the training was going to be canceled. Among our group on the boat,

I almost didn't recognize the kindly psychologist who had assessed me during my pretraining tests. He had shaved his beard, and his smooth face made him look younger. He was studying me, perhaps still trying to figure me out. *An impossible job, Doc,* I thought to myself.

After we clambered aboard the Russian navy training ship, we were given an explanation of the overall training plan. Over the next few days, Dice-K and I were to practice emergency water landings in a mock-up of a *Soyuz* module. Our training was to take place in both a dry setting aboard the ship and in the water. I looked around at the dozens of people who were there to support us—a small army of instructors, medics, and, for no apparent reason, our psychologist.

After the doctors declared us physically and mentally sound, Dice-K and I were shown the training capsule and a large water tank on deck. The tank was filled with brownish seawater covered in dead flies. I sighed. It was even worse than the pool at Star City.

Roaming around the ship during a break, it was obvious that the crew wasn't used to having women aboard. Young recruits smirked and leered. I pretended not to notice and focused on the task ahead. Sevastopol, I believed, was the place to prove I was not a delicate woman who had more money than sense. I wanted to say, *Listen, my Russian friends, I'm no Paris Hilton!*

We were joined by four professional cosmonauts: Fyodor, Oleg, Roman, and Mikhail. Of them, Fyodor was the only one who had flown into space. The rest were rookies just as Dice-K and I were. The difference was they were rookies who had been training for almost seven years. That's all they did, train and train some more. They didn't look particularly pleased to be back for another round of water training.

I was assigned to Fyodor and Oleg's crew. All four cosmonauts spoke English, but Fyodor's was the best since he had spent time in the United

States and even flown on an American space shuttle. Fyodor told me Oleg was an accomplished physician, aerospace engineer, and pilot. He also confided that Oleg was under some pressure since he was scheduled to fly during the next year, and needed to keep his training marks high. The timing and accuracy of the entire crew would determine his grade. That meant I had to do well or Oleg might flunk, which could mean being scrubbed from his flight.

I was nervous but I tried to keep things light by telling jokes, even though I don't usually tell them well, often forgetting the punch lines. Some of the Russian sailors were still watching me with sleazy smiles. Adding to my discomfort, one of the training officers joked to Fyodor and Oleg that they were lucky they had a female in their capsule, because they could undress me.

Fyodor replied, "Maybe lucky for us, but not so lucky for her. If the heat doesn't make her pass out, our body odor will!"

His comment actually put me at ease, because I realized he and Oleg were as nervous about being in the capsule with me as I was with them. I said, "Look, the capsule is like Las Vegas. What happens in the capsule, stays in the capsule."

The cosmonauts stared at me incredulously, then burst out laughing. I thought I could detect a bit of relief on their faces, too.

The capsule training wasn't scheduled until the next day. Before that came the basics. Dice-K and I were ordered to put on black wet suits and prepare for immersion in the water tank. The suits were about three times too big for us, and we came waddling back out on deck looking like shabby penguins.

Dice-K went first. The task was to put on a life vest, climb up a ladder, then fall backward into the tank without bending at the knees. No one explained why we shouldn't bend our knees, but if that's what they wanted, then that's what we would do. Once in the water, we were supposed to inflate our vest by pulling the two red balls hanging from it on lanyards. It took Dice-K three times to accomplish this to the instructors' satisfaction, and then it was my turn. I did it perfectly the first time but was asked to do it again. The second time I bent my knees and wound up repeating the operation four more times until I got it exactly right again. When I finally emerged from the water for the last time, I felt like a failure. I trudged back to the changing room, dripping water and gloom.

That night, Dice-K and I went along with a crowd of training personnel and interpreters to a bowling alley. I called it "disco bowling" because of the fluorescent purple lights and loud music. The next morning, I met the others in the nightclub/dining room for breakfast. Dice-K held his head in his hands and his face matched the color of my oatmeal. I'm sure I didn't look much better. There was a headache lurking and I feared it might get worse. On the ride out to the ship, I sucked in fresh sea air and tried to clear my head. Dice-K sat with his head down. I thought maybe he was going to throw up, but he hung in there. When we climbed aboard the ship, both our legs were wobbly.

The training for the day was in the capsule mock-up on deck. We had to climb inside the capsule while wearing the Sokol suit, remove it, then don a wool sweater, a wool hat, wool overalls, a wool jacket, then another pair of overalls filled with down before finally pulling on a rubber survival suit. Wearing all these layers, we were supposed to exit the capsule onto the ship's deck, waddle over to the water tank, climb its ladder, and fall backward into it, presumably without bending our knees.

Dice-K and his crew went first and crawled inside the capsule. When it started to rain, everyone sought shelter, knowing it would to take a while for the trainees to emerge. Waiting made me anxious so I started some stretching and breathing exercises. Then we were called to an early lunch consisting of a heavy soup, bread, meat, and potatoes.

It was two and a half hours before Dice-K and his crewmates finally emerged from the capsule, soaked with sweat and visibly exhausted. When he fell into the water tank, Dice-K's life vest failed to inflate, so they made him do it again. He crawled out, his face tortured, stood up and flopped backwards into the tank once more. Bobbing up, he pulled the red balls on his vest as hard as he could, but still they did not inflate. While poor Dice-K floundered, the instructors declared the simulation was finished, inflated vest or not. Grateful for small mercies, Dice-K staggered off to his cabin to clean up. He looked so beat, my heart went out to him.

Then it was my turn. I headed for the dressing room. To prepare myself, I braided my hair to keep it out of the way, pulled on the Sokol suit and headed outside. As usual, the suit assigned to me was much too large and I had some difficulty walking. One of the interpreters led me through the corridor and down the ladder to the deck where Oleg and Fyodor were waiting. We were asked to pose for a few pictures, and then Fyodor climbed inside to take the left seat. It had stopped raining and now the sun was very hot. I lowered myself into the capsule and slid over to squeeze into the right seat. I silently thanked my physical trainers back in Star City. They had definitely toughened me up. Assigned as commander for the test, Oleg was next and he made it look easy, swinging inside like an acrobat and settling into the middle seat.

The hatch closed and we put on our seat belts and waited for the command to start the exercise. Oleg explained the order of things. After we got out of our spacesuits and put on all the layers of clothing, he would help Fyodor and me put on our survival suits. Then we would help him. It sounded like a good plan, so when we got word to start, we confidently began to undo our zippers and hooks. Oleg watched me to make sure I was doing everything right, then started to take off his own suit. After getting it off without elbowing me too much, he shoved it down into the little space in front of his seat beneath the instrument panel. He helped me take my arms out of my suit and then asked me to push myself up so he could help me with my legs. Then Oleg turned to assist Fyodor. When I tried to push my suit down into the little empty space in front of my seat, I realized it wasn't as easy as Oleg made it look. That suit just didn't want to go into that hole. Oleg turned to help me and pushed it in with pure force. By this time, we were all sitting in pools of sweat. Oleg turned and knelt backward in his seat. Considering that he was a big, muscular guy, I was amazed by how agile and flexible he was. He was doing things I had only seen before in complicated yoga poses.

I tried to cool Oleg down by pointing my ventilation hose at him while he searched behind the seats for our clothing bundles. I figured since he was doing the bulk of the work, I could at least keep him cool. He handed me my bundle and I put on the sweater—just what was *not* needed, considering how hot it was—and then the wool flight suit. Oleg helped me and Fyodor, and then Fyodor helped Oleg. It was harder for the two Russians since they were bigger and didn't have much room to maneuver. My small size was finally proving to be an advantage.

The next chore was to unpack a cold-water immersion suit and put it on. The suit was made of heavy rubber and did not go on easily. To get into it we had to zip up all the other layers of clothes, making things even hotter. I pulled myself up in the seat and stood, bending over and grabbing the suit to put my legs in, but there just wasn't enough room. Oleg told me to stretch my legs in front of him and he would help. I hung with both arms from the hatch while he tried to stuff me inside the suit. He then helped me push my head through the rubber dam and tighten the strap to make the suit watertight. Oleg laughed and said a video of all this would make good stuff for the paparazzi. I laughed with him, but I also worried about being a burden since he was helping me so much. When it came time to zip the thing up, I realized its zipper was broken. I tried to fix it but Oleg told me not to worry about it and leave it alone.

By then, it was deathly hot in the capsule. After squeezing myself into a corner, I kept pointing my ventilation hose at my crewmates as they struggled into their immersion suits. When they were finally suited up, Oleg located the emergency kits for each of us, handed them out, and asked if we were ready. Close to heat exhaustion, Fyodor and I eagerly nodded. Oleg informed the instructors we were coming out and then opened the hatch. He emerged first and I followed. The first flush of fresh air in hours felt delicious. I waddled over to the tank, climbed up and fell backwards into the water, keeping my knees as straight as possible. After Fyodor got in, cameras clicked and whirred, and the three of us posed victoriously. Despite its broken zipper, my suit hadn't leaked much.

We were given a little time to take a much-needed shower before reporting for a debriefing. Everyone was there: the instructors, the beardless psychologist, the doctors, the interpreters, and most of the ship's officers and crew. When we were asked to describe our experiences, I was pleased when Oleg and Fyodor said I had done really well. When my turn came, I thanked them for all their help and mentioned my broken zipper. This was a mistake. An instructor, with a deadly serious expression, wanted to know if I had broken it. I swore it was already broken and Oleg backed me up. Still, I saw a few frowns and wished I hadn't said anything. Another lesson learned.

We went back to our hotel, freshened up, and then Dice-K, our trainers, and a couple of the cosmonauts went to a sushi bar for dinner. Dice-K was excited to have some Japanese food and helped us through the 30-page menu to pick the best dishes. I don't recall if sake was served but there was inevitably plenty of vodka. Dice-K, I noticed, didn't drink as much as he had on the other nights.

The next day, we repeated the survival training, this time with the capsule in the water. Unluckily for us trainees, a storm had swept through the night before and the sea was filled with waves. Nevertheless, and even though it was again deathly hot in the capsule, it was somehow easier to get into and out of everything. In near record time, Oleg, Fyodor, and I happily exited the bobbing capsule. When I fell backward into the sea, I figured out why we were told not to bend our knees. When you bend your knees, you naturally push down as you go out, instead of just falling backward. Pushing down on the open hatch of the *Soyuz* while it's bobbing on the water could cause it to flood, which is obviously not a good thing.

After being fished out, I felt like I had accomplished everything in fine fashion and hoped the instructors were also pleased. I wondered if I would have to go through the Sevastopol survivor training again if I was ever assigned a flight. I hoped not. But when I thought it over, I decided if I had to, I'd just do it even better next time.

What I didn't know was not only had the instructors been quite pleased with my progress, but the wheel of fate was turning and it was about to change everything. In fact, what was heading my way was nothing less than an old-fashioned, honest-to-goodness miracle.

June 1, 2006, was our last day of training in Sevastopol. The next day, we took a bus excursion to Yalta, the famous Black Sea resort. On the way, I contemplated my emotional state. All my nerves were rubbed raw, but not in a bad way. I was savoring the smallest things such as the perfume of flowers, the taste of food, the kind smile of someone trying to help. Quite simply, I had never felt so alive.

The first place we visited was a church overlooking the villa where So-viet President Mikhail Gorbachev was kept under house arrest during the collapse of the USSR. It was a beautiful spot. Roman, our interpreter, told us churchgoers came there to light candles for loved ones who had passed away. I lit two, one for my Buhbuh and one for Uncle Frank. I told them both how much I missed them and that they would always be in my heart. I also told them I hoped they were proud of me for what I was doing. Feel-ing peaceful, I stayed there until the others came after me to continue on.

When we reached Yalta, we stopped at a stone beach and a castle called the Bird's Nest. Everyone else went for a swim but I decided it was too cold, so I walked the beach collecting rocks to pretty up a vase of bamboo in my Prophy apartment. We were all hungry and a plate of small fish along with some beer was delivered. Since I don't drink alcohol, I substituted mineral water. I inspected the fish and was turned off. They had been fried whole—heads, tails, guts, everything. When hunger finally got the best of me, I tried one and found it to be absolutely delicious. I probably had about half a dozen.

Next, we headed to a restaurant near the castle with a gorgeous view of the Black Sea. Vodka, beer, and mineral water quickly arrived and the tradi-tional toasts began. First, the captain of the training ship presented the cos-monauts, Dice-K, and me with photographs of us in the water during the training. The cosmonauts stood up and thanked the entire team for all their help and support. Fyodor even made a toast in my honor, said some very kind words about me, and then, to my astonishment, everyone in the room stood up and raised their glasses to me! My face felt hot and I realized I was blushing furiously!

Then they asked Dice-K to say something and I knew I would be next. I quickly started thinking of what to say. When my turn came, I stood up, nervous as a schoolgirl, raised my glass and made a toast to the beautiful weather, delicious food, cold vodka, and new friends. Afterwards, I heard that everyone liked that I tried to say the toast in Russian. Sometimes, I have learned, it is the little things that make the most difference to others.

When, to their embarrassment, the cosmonauts came up a bit short of cash while paying for our lunch, I cheerfully helped them out. As we were walking to the bus, Oleg and Fyodor told me how terrible they felt about sticking me with part of the bill. I replied it was no problem, but they said everyone wanted to do something to make up for it. I kept telling them not to worry, that everything was fine, and it was.

On the drive back to Sevastopol, we stopped for what I thought was a break and nearly everyone got off the bus. I stayed, talking to Roman the interpreter. Roman's accounts of his experiences with the other Space Adventures travelers, including Dennis Tito, Mark Shuttleworth, and Greg Olsen, were always fascinating, and he was in the middle of one of his stories when Fyodor and Oleg returned, carrying a beautiful bouquet of red roses. When they said they were for me, my eyes welled with tears and I wanted to hug them for being so sweet. These two accomplished men really, genuinely cared for me, and I felt so fortunate to be in their company. I hoped they could sense how I felt because there was no way for me to adequately express it in words.

When we arrived at the hotel, everyone changed for another celebratory party. To let everyone know how much I appreciated them, I arranged with the hotel to pay for everything. After drinks were poured, Oleg and Fyodor toasted me anew and asked me to say something. After I told them in Russian how much I appreciated their friendship and support, everyone stood up and cheered. The party ended before midnight and I headed upstairs to pack. For just a moment, I gave myself a moment to reflect. The training at Sevastapol had been a wonderful experience, and I had made friends for life.

✦ ✦ ✦

Back in Star City, the days of training blurred together. It was a warm summer and I gloried in the sunshine and got outside every chance I could. My first weightless training took place in late July on a big jet aircraft that had most of its seats removed, leaving a big open space in which to move around. To simulate weightlessness requires the plane to fly up at a steep angle and then over the top. On the way down, the occupants are falling, thus simulating what the astronauts and cosmonauts call the zero-G of space. Before we went up, Dice-K and I were given heavy parachutes and some quick training on how to jump out of the back of the plane if things went very wrong. I told myself this plane better not crash because there was no way I was going to jump. Fortunately, I didn't have to. In fact, the ride was spectacular. It was wonderful to sail weightlessly across the aircraft although I didn't much care for the extra g-forces at the bottom of each dive. I also managed to not throw up, although everyone thought I would. Dice-K turned a sickly green, but also managed to control himself and finish the training. I felt so bad for him. While I was having fun doing somersaults he looked like he couldn't wait for it to be over.

One of our training sessions required Dice-K and me to venture into the woods surrounding Star City for outdoor survival training. This training was supposed to prepare us in case we landed in a remote backwoods and had to survive on our own until rescue. I quickly got the hang of making a tent out of my parachute, building a fire, and even shooting a gun. It was all a great deal of fun, and I thought that maybe when I got back Hamid and I should take up camping. Dice-K did fine but it was pretty clear he didn't care for being outdoors. He didn't like being hot or cold, and he hated bugs. I didn't see a single bug in Russia that could match the roaches I'd fought in Tehran, so they didn't faze me in the least.

Finally, it was August. There was one class after another and one simulation after the next. Although I longed for Hamid, I had settled into a pleasant routine and was really quite happy. Still, there was always the unsettling fear that I was doing all this for nothing. My requests to join Peggy and Yuri on their flight had come to nothing. I thought it would be years before I had a chance to fly. Then, to my astonishment, all that changed.

It was around 4:30 in the afternoon on August 21. I had just finished my last class and was in a car with Misha, my Space Adventures driver, going into Moscow to meet Hamid, who had managed to break away from business to help me pack for my trip back to Dallas. When my cell phone rang, it was Eric Anderson from Space Adventures. He said, "You've probably heard the news." When I said I hadn't, he replied, "Dice-K has been disqualified due to medical reasons, and you've been moved up to the primary crew for Expedition 14."

When the words sank in, I was in total shock. "Are you joking?"

"I'm serious," Eric replied.

I still couldn't grasp it. "Is this for real?"

"Yes, yes," he answered, impatiently. "Of course, there will be an official panel to discuss the change with the primary crew members and also the managers in Star City. But if they approve, you are good to go. Do you want to go?"

I started screaming, "Are you kidding me? *Of course I want to go!*"

My next thought was for Dice-K. I asked about him and Eric said, "He knows. He was with the doctors all day. He is not completely out of the program. He just needs to take care of some medical issues and then he can return. We'll work to fly him as soon as possible."

I felt a strange mix of emotions. I was elated, of course, but I also felt guilty for taking Dice-K's place. I knew how disappointed I would feel if something like that had happened to me. But then—and I apologize for this—I felt a sense of overwhelming joy.

When Eric rang off, I told Misha what had happened. He slammed the brakes on the car, gave me a big hug, and said he had prayed for me to go. More calls poured in—Akane, Marsel—everyone congratulating me. My heart thudded in my chest so hard, I could feel it in my temples. I started telling myself, "Anousheh, you *cannot* have a heart attack now!" After I had calmed myself down, I thought about what needed to be done.

Three weeks! That's all the time I had to prepare myself to go into space. Was there time to do everything I wanted to do? Most of all, I wanted all my family to come and see me go into space. When I told Akane, she said that it would be difficult but possible if I got all the passport information to the Russians within the next few days. I finally got through to Hamid and told him—no, screamed at him—"I'm going!"

Calmly, my dear husband replied, "I knew you would. I felt it."

I said, "You have made my dream come true!"

Just as in our favorite movie, *The Princess Bride,* he replied with a chuckle, "As you wish."

Hamid was waiting for me at the hotel. I was so glad to see him and so excited, I literally threw myself into his arms and covered him with kisses. I kept thanking him over and over for making it all possible. Later, as I lay in his arms, I thought of Atousa, Amir, my mom and dad, Uncle Frank, Aunt Chamsi, and my Buhbuh and Maman, all of whom had helped me so much. I silently thanked them and thought, "I'm going now. I'm going because *of* you and *for* you." I like to think they all heard me.

A Patch of Trouble

*T*hree weeks until flight!

Being told that I would be flying into space in three weeks was outrageous, amazing, and wonderful all at once. Suddenly, it seemed as if everyone in the world wanted to know everything about me. To create a Web site about my flight for the media and people everywhere, Amir and Terri Griffin, Prodea's vice president of marketing, worked for 48 straight hours. Hamid flew back to Texas and started putting together the logistics required to get visas for everyone in the family so they could come to the launch. To pull all the publicity together, Terri also began to work with Stacey Tearne, who handled public relations for Space Adventures. I liked both of these women. Between them, I knew they could handle anything.

Energia, the manufacturer of both the *Soyuz* rocket and the space capsule, held a small ceremony for me. After a couple of nice speeches from dignitaries, the president of Energia presented me with an official cosmonaut wristwatch, which I had coveted ever since watching Dice-K get his. It was a big watch with lots of knobs, perfect for a man with muscular arms who stood maybe six feet tall. Despite this, I absolutely adored it and refused to take it off.

After a few days, I had a conference call with Terri and Stacey, along with representatives of Space Adventures and the X Prize, to see how we might accomplish a few important things. First, I wanted to have the means during my spaceflight to convey the message to people around the world that dreams, no matter how big, could come true if one was willing to work for them and never give up. I also wanted to be able to stress the importance of science, education, and spaceflight to the younger generations around the world. I didn't know if I would be allowed to communicate while up there, but if I could, that's what I wanted.

The conference call also included a discussion of experiments I might do while on board the Space Station. I recognized that there would not be enough time for me to take any of the experiments I wanted, in particular a telescope for student and amateur astronomers to use remotely. Hardware like that took years to design and be approved for spaceflight. A representative from Space Adventures suggested I take over the experiments that Dice-K was going to do for the European Space Agency. I agreed, but still wanted something unique. Then, Peter Diamandis, who was in on the teleconference, came up with a great idea. "Why don't you do a blog from space, Anousheh? What better way to inspire people and educate them about space? Write about it at the same time you're experiencing it."

When I questioned whether I could write well enough, Peter told me, "Sure you can. Just write whatever comes to your mind." Terri jumped in and said she would work with Peter to set it all up. There were a lot of technical issues to be solved with the Russians and NASA, but I was confident Terri and Peter would get everything done. I hung up feeling much better about everything, and ready to journey to Kazakhstan, where my rocket awaited me.

ᢣ᠊ᢗ᠊ᢒᠻᠵᠻᢗᢣ

A NOTE FROM TERRI GRIFFIN

Aside from the general coordinator role, Anousheh gave me the responsibility of finding a PR firm to handle publicity outreach, so I started looking around, beginning with some companies that Space Adventures and the X Prize people recommended. They were all very expensive, but I finally negotiated one down to a merely outrageous amount. The guy in charge proved to be ineffective. Anousheh really wanted to be on The Oprah Winfrey Show *because she knew millions of women watched it and she wanted to reach them, especially women living in closed societies. The PR guy said maybe he could get Anousheh in* Vanity Fair *and* Cosmopolitan *magazines, but she should forget about Oprah. Finally, he asked, "Did you really think anyone was going to be interested in another rich person going into space?" That was the end of our working relationship.*

Fortunately, I also had Cynthia Stine of the Promote Success agency in Dallas working on the side, and in no time at all, they'd made contact with Oprah's people. After a lot of back and forth, we came to terms. Anousheh would be on Oprah *shortly after her flight, as long as she didn't go on another show first.*

Another responsibility I had was coordinating Anousheh's communications from space. The X Prize people wanted her to talk to students at the International Space University, Massachusetts Institute of Technology, and St. Louis Science Center. Space Adventures wanted her to address potential clients. Of course, we also had lots of media requests, so I started working to set up live interviews through the Russian link. Anousheh had her own requests as well, primarily to talk to the employees of her company and to children and other school kids through the ham radio on board. On top of

*all that, she wanted time to talk to her family. It was a lot to juggle,
and I had to clear everything with the Russians and NASA. During this time, I was also getting hundreds of e-mails from private
citizens. Most were encouraging and nice, but some were crazy people who thought little green men in space existed and wanted
Anousheh to talk to them on their behalf. I had fun showing those
to my kids just to let them see how nutty some people could be at
times. Many people simply wanted money. I remember one e-mail
I got that said only this:"SEND ME SOM MONY!!!" I still laugh
when I think about that one.*

⁂

Although the Expedition 14 crew learned I was going to be part of their crew on
Friday, it took until Monday for me to catch up with them. Misha greeted
me warmly but the NASA astronaut, Michael Lopez-Alegria (whom most
called L. A.), was difficult to read. L. A. was a familiar face. I had often seen
him at Star City during classes. He nearly always wore his military uniform
while most of us wore jeans and t-shirts, and I rarely saw him smile. The
first time I'd actually seen L. A. was on the big IMAX screen in the film
Space Station, about the building, launching, and assembly of the international outpost. L. A. was on the first assembly missions, before they even
turned on the lights. While watching the movie, I would have never in a million years thought I would actually meet Michael Lopez-Alegria, much less
fly into space with him.

I found Misha and L. A. practicing in a *Soyuz* simulator. When they
finished their lesson, they climbed out, congratulated me, and expressed
concern for Dice-K. It was obvious they hadn't been told why he was off
the flight. I told them what I knew, that it had to do with an illness, and

that maybe Dice-K might yet be allowed to fly. The two absorbed this information and went back to their training. A day later I saw them again, this time during the first of two simulations required before flight, something like a final exam. For this simulation, which had to do with the launch sequence, we were presented with three envelopes, each holding different malfunctions for us to resolve. Misha, as the *Soyuz* commander, was supposed to choose the envelope, but he asked me to do it. It turned out to be a good choice as the malfunctions thrown at us were easy. The next day, I also chose the envelope. My choice this time was not as good. A couple of hours into the simulation, we were told there was a fire aboard the station that had to be put out.

Fires in space are one of the worst things that can happen. There had been a fire on the old Russian space station *Mir* that raged for hours and nearly suffocated the crew. To put out the fire in our simulation, we had to go into the Russian segment of the ISS mockup, don bulky gas masks, fight the fire, and then evacuate the area. It was hot in there, and the lenses in the gas masks of both my crewmates quickly fogged over. For some reason, my mask remained clear, and I was able to read the emergency procedures to them out loud. Both men complimented me, telling me they were glad I was with them and that I'd impressed them by keeping my cool in what could have been a bad situation.

After our final exams, it was time to go to Baikonur in Kazakhstan for two weeks of quarantine prior to launch. Before we left, I learned of a comment L. A. had made to a reporter, saying, "I'm not a big fan, personally, of having those guys go visit the space station because I think the space station is still a place that is under construction and not quite operational. I don't think it's ideal."

"Those guys" referred to me and the other Space Adventure participants. I could have gotten upset about his opinion, but I didn't. He had a right to it and I had other problems to solve. One of them had to do with the patches I wanted to wear on my spacesuit and my work coveralls.

Nearly everyone who has flown into space goes with specially designed patches and logos sewn on their suits. At a minimum, these include a national flag and a mission patch. For Expedition 14, our mission patch consisted of the roman numeral XIV against a black background containing five stars that represented the five missions when astronauts and cosmonauts lost their lives. Below the black sky and the stars was the blue and white hemisphere of Earth. It was a lovely patch, and I admired it even though I was not allowed to wear it. I was not, you see, officially part of the mission, but simply a guest of the Russians. Earlier on, when I was still a backup, I decided it would be a good thing to have my own patch when and if I had a chance to fly, and had worked on its design until I was satisfied. Now that I was going into space, I wanted to wear my patch. I also wanted to wear both the American and Iranian flags. Iran was my homeland and I thought it was important to recognize that fact as a sign of respect for my relatives and the people of Iran. The resulting uproar from both the Russian and American space agencies plus the international media was absolutely incredible. You would have thought I was going to carry a bomb into orbit rather than a couple of pieces of cloth.

Problems with my patches had come up even before I was assigned to a flight. A reporter covering one of my training sessions noted in a story that I had the flag of Iran sewn on my coveralls. The next thing I knew the chief of the Russian training program himself was telling me I couldn't make a political statement and had to remove the flag. I was astonished and argued that I was a completely apolitical person and was only trying to represent the country of my birth. Anyway, I explained, my patch wasn't the actual Iranian flag, just three innocent little bars that happened to be red, white, and green. The official flag of Iran has those bars, but also an emblem in its center in the shape of the name of Allah and "God is Great" in Arabic 22 times along the flag's border. I thought my argument was a good one, but the Russian chief said he didn't care, the patch had to come off. I removed the patch to avoid trouble, since I thought it would be years before I flew anyway. I would fight the battle later if it became necessary.

With my hurry-up assignment to Expedition 14, the patch problem came up again. This time, it had to do with my personal patch, a design I was sure would not be controversial. Along the top border were the words *Imagine, Be the Change,* and *Inspire.* In the center was a drawing of the space station and emerging from it was a human figure with curved arms that turned into the symbol for infinity. Below this were the words *Soyuz,* the vehicle that would carry me into space, and *TMA–9,* the number of the launch. Beneath these words, in small triangles, were the colors of the flags of the United States and Iran. At the very bottom was my name, *Anousheh Ansari.* Naturally, it was that one tiny little triangle with the Iranian colors that caused the outcry.

Once more, the head of Russian training came to me and said not only could I not have the Iranian flag on any of my suits, but my personal patch had to go as well. I was angry and after being encouraged by some American astronauts who reminded me we Americans have freedom of speech *and* freedom of religion, I wrote a letter to NASA administrator Mike Griffin for help. He never answered the letter, but one person who stepped up was Rick Tumlinson, the cofounder of the respected Space Frontier Foundation. Of my situation with the patches, he told a reporter for MSNBC, "It's the stupidest damn thing I've ever heard. We're missing a tremendous opportunity to deliver a message to the real Iranian people. She should wear Iran's flag on her suit and our people should be proclaiming the fact that an Iranian woman, oppressed in her own country, can come here and make a fortune and spend it by pursuing her dream, enabled by an American company working with the Russians to fly her into space."

Naturally, I agreed, but it didn't matter. I was told there were 16 countries paying for the space station, and Iran wasn't one of them. This went back and forth for a while but, finally recognizing I was outnumbered, I agreed to remove my patches. However, I had a backup plan. My flight coveralls had already been sent to be packed aboard the *Soyuz* and my personal patch was sewn onto them. My hope was they had been forgotten. I knew my personal patch and an Iranian flag had also already been sewn on my Sokol suit and hoped they'd forgotten about that, too. But a couple of days before I flew I was told the patch was coming off. That's when I came up with the idea of just sewing white thread over the green color in the tiny triangle in the corner of my patch. The Russians agreed, and it was actually done! I still have a mental image of some big, tough Russian technician using a tiny needle and white thread to make me politically correct.

To begin our 14 days of quarantine prior to flight, Misha, L. A., Yuri, Peggy, and I flew to Kazakhstan and moved into the Cosmonaut Hotel. Despite its grand name, it was an old two-story building that looked like a cheap motel. Our rooms, simple and clean, were on the second floor with shared bathrooms. I shared a two-bedroom suite with Peggy. The best thing about the hotel was that it had wireless Internet, provided by NASA. While in quarantine, I would at least have contact with the outside world.

A friend sent me an e-mail with a photograph of me in the Sokol suit and told me it had appeared on the official Iranian Space Agency Web site. Since Iranian women still have to keep their hair covered, I was astonished to see my hair in the photograph. It didn't take long before I got another e-mail showing the same photograph, again on the Iranian Space Agency site, except this time it had been digitally manipulated to cover my hair with a helmet. It all sort of amused me. I imagine that someone in the agency had gotten into a little trouble over the first picture. Overall, the press and reports from Iran were positive. It was wonderful to know that millions of Iranians were following my journey into space. In a very real way, I felt like I had reconnected with my home country.

There were many articles about my flight where reporters called me a "space tourist." The first chance I got when talking to the media, I tried to correct this misconception by saying, "I take offense when they call me a 'tourist,' because the image is of someone with a camera around their neck and a ticket in their hand walking into the airport to go on a trip somewhere and coming back to show their pictures. My flight into space is much more than that." I added, "Look, I've been training for six months. If you want to compare my experience on Earth, it's probably closer to expeditions where scientists go to Antarctica or mountaineers climb Mount Everest. Those kinds of things, just like my flight, require a lot more preparation, thinking, and studying than tourists on a tour." Sadly, my objections were ignored. "Space tourist" seemed to become part of my name: "Space tourist Anousheh Ansari" this and "Space tourist Anousheh Ansari" that.

⁂

Back home in Texas, Hamid and Terri were being hounded by the press, mostly about my patch problem. "We definitely don't want to dilute the message with politics," Hamid assured a reporter and then went on to explain that I was a space fanatic. "It's part of her DNA," he said. "It's in her." But when the reporter wouldn't let go of the politics, Hamid said, in exasperation, "She's from Iran no matter what. Wearing a flag or not wearing a flag doesn't change where we were born. I think we worry about the semantics too much and that the whole message is getting lost." The message, of course, being, "Be the dream that you want to be, basically," as Hamid said. He was absolutely correct.

Then, NBC News space analyst James Oberg chimed in with a posting on an Internet discussion board, wondering if I was going to cause problems with the upcoming Islamic holy month of Ramadan. He wrote, "The first day of Ramadan this year is expected to be September 24, following a sighting the previous evening of the crescent new moon by observant Muslims. But it's possible that Ansari's unique position in space may allow her to spot the crescent a day earlier, and if she reports it credibly, the entire Muslim world may have to start Ramadan a day earlier than expected."

When Oberg called and asked me about it, I said, "To be honest with you, I will be observing the moon as many times as I can, because I think it's a beautiful view up there. It makes it that much more special, knowing that it's a very special time for Muslims around the world." It was the best I could do, and Oberg seemed to like my answer. I just hoped he would drop that whole angle. I was simply not going to be responsible for Ramadan!

⁕⁂⁕

One of the first things we did upon arrival in Baikonur was to raise the flags of our respective countries outside the Cosmonaut Hotel. This was one of many traditions the Russians have before a crew goes into orbit. With our backups Peggy and Yuri, we prime crew members assembled at three flagpoles on a little grassy spot. Then, a big group of blue-shirted soldiers wearing wide saucer-shaped hats marched out to salute as one Russian and two American flags were hoisted. Although Misha and I were bareheaded, L. A. wore his United States Navy cap. When the flags went up, he delivered a perfect salute.

We then began our life in the Cosmonaut Hotel. We rose each day at 6 a.m., had medical checks by a doctor who came to our rooms, exercised, ate breakfast, called family and friends, read and sent e-mail, had lunch, perhaps did some interviews, more calls, more e-mail, some recap training, then dinner, and to bed. Day in, day out. I kept thinking of the Bill Murray movie *Groundhog Day*.

The kitchen was off-limits to crew members, so we had to present ourselves in the hotel's small dining room at designated times for our meals. We couldn't leave the premises and could only walk around under supervision. While it felt at times like a minimum-security prison, the truth was that I would have slept in the mud and eaten gruel to go into space. In fact, I was content in my quarantine, even though time ticked by slowly. Hamid gave me a stack of DVDs when he came to see me off to Baikonur, and on most nights, we gathered in either L. A.'s or Misha's room and watched the movies.

As the days passed, I saw and heard only a little of the reporting about my flight but kept up as best I could through e-mail and telephone calls. One article that I particularly liked was by Heather Mayer of Radio Free Europe, who asked Atousa if I was nervous. Atousa replied, "She's not nervous, actually. She's very excited. I think she's just, right now, very excited to get up there and go, as I am."

I was so proud of my sister for setting the correct tone for my flight. She was absolutely right. I wasn't nervous at all. I was counting the minutes and hours.

A few days after my arrival, I began to write my blog. I was self-conscious about it at first but tried to stick to Peter's concept and write down what was going through my mind. Amazingly, it turned out that people enjoyed reading what I wrote and before long, I got word that the audience on my Web site was growing.

From all the evidence, I was still getting good press in Iran. My story was featured in the big Iranian newspapers, *Hambastegi* and *Jam-e-Jam Daily*. An Iranian astronomer and science journalist named Pouria Nazemi interviewed me and published a very complimentary article in the magazine *NOJUM*. The Iranian state television channel also aired a telephone conversation between Mr. Nazemi and me for an entire hour. On the program, Mr. Nazemi recommended that all Iranians gather at night to watch me when the ISS passed over Iran's cities. Another Iranian, Shahram Yazdanpanah, posted about me on his space science Web site. Mr. Nazemi and Mr. Yazdanpanah kept everything nonpolitical, and I couldn't have been more pleased.

But the coverage was not all sweetness and light. Some newspaper and magazine articles in Iran were critical. One said my flight was a bad example for young Iranian women because I was not following Islamic laws in my appearance or conduct. Another chided me for using my wealth to fly to space rather than help the poor. They apparently made no attempt to discover that Hamid and I were actually big contributors to a number of charities. I tried not to take any of the criticisms personally. I knew a public figure had to have a thick skin, but it was hard at times.

Inadvertently, I gave a funny interview to Alan Boyle of MSNBC. When he asked if I was aware of any changes that had been made by the Russians to accommodate me, I gave this answer:

> Well, the only modification that I'm aware of is the modification to the toilet they had to make. The toilet is not a very convenient contraption to use to start with, but there is a funnel at the top of it that people use for urination. And in addition to the funnel, they needed to have another female adapter for the top of the toilet system. That's the only thing I'm aware of, unless there's something else I'm not *privy* to.

English is my third language and I don't know all the colloquialisms. I wasn't aware of the other meaning of *privy!*

I was also very pleased to hear L. A.'s reply to a reporter's question at a news conference held shortly after our arrival in Baikonur. These were conducted behind a wall of glass so the reporters couldn't breathe on us and spread germs. When asked how comfortable he was to fly with a "space tourist" like me, L. A. confessed he had been skeptical of private participants in space, but it was now clear the Russian space program needed the money. He went on to say that Anousheh Ansari going into space "is a great dream and a great hope, not just for our country, but for countries all around the world." Misha went further, calling me "very professional," and adding that it seemed we had worked together for a decade already.

I attributed L. A.'s apparent change of heart to his having gotten to know me as a person rather than assuming I was a rich woman who wanted to go to space on a whim. We had many discussions about my dreams of the stars and why I sponsored the X Prize, and what I hoped to accomplish with my spaceflight. I don't know that he was completely convinced, but I think he came to accept that I believed I was doing the right thing.

✦

My fortieth birthday was September 12, six days prior to our scheduled launch. When the doctor came to my room that morning to take my resting heart rate and blood pressure, he brought with him some wildflowers he had picked on his way to the Cosmonaut Hotel. He wished me a happy birthday, took his measurements, and left. As far as I knew, that would be the extent of any celebration. Everyone at Baikonur was so busy. Anyway, I had already received the best gift possible: the chance to go into space. I got ready and went down to exercise and then came back to my room to take a quick peek at my e-mails. There were quite a few from family and friends wishing me happiness on my special day. The best one was from Hamid, who made it clear he thought I was the most beautiful 40-year-old woman in the world. If I could have changed myself into electrons, I would have gone soaring through the ether to wrap myself around him just like they do on *Star Trek*.

When I opened the door to go to breakfast, I was surprised to see someone had hung a big poster of me covered in birthday wishes. At breakfast, there was a huge arrangement of red roses and a specially baked apple pie on the table. General Valeri Korzun, a former cosmonaut and deputy chief of the Cosmonaut Training Center, walked in with the head of the Baikonur training program and presented me with a large basket of white roses. Throughout the day, it seemed everyone I encountered gave me birthday wishes and flowers. Yuri Malenchenko even gave me gladiolas.

Since it is the tradition in Russia that the person having the birthday throws a party, I arranged a little beer fest after dinner. Besides Misha, L. A., Peggy, and Yuri, our training team was also invited. Soon, everyone was toasting me. The best toast was from Misha, who said, "You are who you show without disguise and pretensions, and that is why we all enjoy working with you." He then invited me to officially join the cosmonaut corps. Tears of gratitude formed in my eyes as he spoke. I was so moved I even danced a traditional Kazakh dance with General Korzun!

I continued to send out my blog on the X Prize Web site and also on my own fledgling domain, www.anoushehansari.com. Terri reported many thousands of hits. I was amazed when comments poured in from around the world, nearly all positive. It was especially delightful when they were from Iran:

Hi Anoushe joon

Happy birthday

Just wanted to let you know as an Iranian woman that I am proud of you and congradulate you for your up high dreams and achivement of this adventure

Kiss the face of infinity for me, and say hi to the moonlight. I can not wait to hear your story when you come back.

I wish a happy happy time during your stay, and I wish your unique host (The Orbit) make you the best memories, my prayers go with you during your historic trip.*

I'm a teenager from Iran with lots of dreams. I'll have a very difficult year this year . . . but as you said "Even for the most impossible dream, there is always a way to make it come true . . ." I want to enter university this year with best grades. I know I can do it. If you like remember my name. I am Ali Mohammadi. Although I don't know anything about space but I want to continue my study in space engineering. God help you to be more successful, you are young Iranian hope.

Best wishes, Ali**

---

* http://www.anoushehansari.com/blog/091206.php#comment-30
** http://www.anoushehansari.com/blog/091206.php#comment-141

Dear Anousheh,

As an Iranian woman I'm really really proud of you. You are a role model not only for Iranian women but also for every woman in the world. I wish you an enjoyable trip to your dreams and a safe return to earth. Oh my god . . . isn't that exciting? you're gonna fly to heaven, I can hear my heartbeat thinking about that!*

May God bless Anousheh and the Crew. Lets treat everybody human. It is interesting and happy to see an Iranian born girl with American passport travelling through Russian shuttle/rocket from Kazakhstan to the International station. More over she is getting a chance to see her home (earth-family) as a whole. If her $20 million spending can make me to write like this then you achieved your goal I should say. Thanks God bless not only America, everybody in EARTH.**

But there were also a number of comments that were negative, such as these:

I was watching interview with Anousheh Ansari from channel 4—Night Sky program—a phone conversation from Kazakhstan. I had read about her before and about the X Prize too. First I did envy her because of her experience in space, but when I saw how much she has paid—$20 million—I thought how many children

---

* http://www.anoushehansari.com/blog/091306.php#comment-113
**http://cosmiclog.msnbc.msn.com/archive/2006/09/15/4080.aspx

could be saved from dying with this money. Oh God! I would do many other things, if I was her . . . *

Hi

I want to honest with you.

1. you r looking for fame, becuase you r missing something so dearly, let me guess you don't have any children
2. like all Iranian you like to show off, that is why you want to be the first Irannian in space
3. If I had money I would be Milanda Gates, not Anousheh Ansari, Because fighting cancer make more sence than wasting money in space
4. Sorry for being so hard, but look for inner satisfaction, rather than searching for it in space.**

Hi

congratulation for your success as first space tourist for space.

It is private matter who and how spend his or her time and life BUT Do we if we know many peopl suffer from diseases, many

---

* http://www.anoushehansari.com/blog/091306.php#comment-81
** http://www.anoushehansari.com/blog/091606.php#comment-422

doesn't have any thing to eat, many try end their life because they cant't afford to buy something for their family.

Any way we don't live in a fair world, why should we care about others? we live as like as we want and enjoy!but many can't.

may be here is not place to say this,sorry for unreleveant comments.for me the best thing to do is to do some thing to re-life some one form pain.

enjoy your trip, have fun*

ℐ⟩⥽⋆⥼ℂ⟩ℐ

I admit the comments stung. I sat for a long time reading them, all the while feeling unfairly judged. I decided to present my point of view in my blog. After giving it a lot of thought, I titled the entry "Price of a Dream," and wrote:

How do you put a price on your Dream? Is it worth one month's salary? Is it worth one year's salary? . . . What is the right price for a dream?

I don't have an answer for it. But I believe it is different for every person. For me, I was ready, and still am, to give my life for my dream. . . .

Where did my money come from? From hard work, an incredible amount of risk, and many sacrifices that my family and I

---

* http://spaceblog.xprize.org/2006/09/13/training-as-backup/#comment-104

had to make. Do we have the right to decide what to do with this hard-earned money? I would think so! Does this mean that I'm selfish and do not care about all the suffering that goes on in the world? Well, I must say that you need to get to know me better and decide for yourself. . . .

Personally, I almost always focus on long-term fundamental activities that address the root causes of a problem. . . . Did you know that space research helps figure out changes in soil conditions and environment and ways of preventing crop damage?

. . . I also think many people go hungry not because there is a lack of food or help from other countries but because of the lack of honest and effective systems to get the food in the hands of those hungry children. The only way we can change this is through education of our youth to become free thinkers. . . . This is also a message that I'm trying to send to the world.

I support organizations like the X Prize and Ashoka Foundation because they are not about making a difference in a small community. These organizations are about Changing the World and making it a better place to live for everyone.

What is the price of a dream? For me, it is putting my life and my money where my mouth is.*

I finished writing and resolutely pushed the send button. Now my hopes, dreams, purpose, and passion were out there for everyone to see and judge. Would the naysayers be convinced? I decided it didn't matter. As I sat in my dark little room in the Cosmonaut Hotel in deepest Kazakhstan with only

---

* http://www.anoushehansari.com/blog/091406.php

the glow of my laptop for illumination, I concluded that nothing I could say would ever convince everyone. I believed I was doing the right thing, and that was the most I could hope for. And so, as the clock ticked steadily toward my personal rendezvous with destiny, I dedicated myself anew to the stars.

Into Space

*T*he persistent chirping of the alarm on my official cosmonaut wristwatch brought me out of a fitful sleep the day before my flight. It was still hard for me to believe where I was and what I was about to do. I also feared a last-minute glitch. With all the controversies over my patches, Ramadan, my hair, what happened to Dice-K, and everything else, I didn't think I was being paranoid. I halfway expected at any moment to be drawn aside and told I was out. It was like a persistent demon of doom sitting on my shoulder whispering into my ear.

I wanted to get up but I had to stay in bed until a doctor came to measure my resting blood pressure. After fidgeting for what seemed like hours but was probably only a few minutes, the door opened to reveal the face of a Russian flight surgeon. He put the BP cuff on me, saying, "*Dobrey Odrom, kak sama chousteh?*" which means, "Good morning. How do you feel?" I replied, probably sounding defensive, "*Kharashow* [Good]." I could feel my heart accelerating, and I was sure he was going to say my BP was too high or too low, or that my heart rate was erratic. I looked into his eyes, willing him to speak. Finally he smiled and said, "*Vcyeu normalna* [Everything is normal]." I sighed with relief.

The doctor wished me a good day and left. I climbed out of bed and stood at my window, staring at the sliver of bright orange on the horizon announcing the coming day. Looking back at me was a reflection in the glass of a small woman who, at that moment, seemed to be hanging by a thread. Was the world ready for an Iranian, even one who had become an American citizen, to fly into space? Might it cause some delicate international diplomacy I wasn't even aware of to be turned on its head? Were there forces out there who were dedicated to stopping me from fulfilling my life's dream?

I told the demon of gloom that seemed to be whispering into my ear to shut up and go away. It was difficult to explain, even to myself, this strange mix of excitement and anxiety, except to confess again I think it's in my Iranian genes to worry. I demanded of the reflection in the window, "Is it worth it?" The answer came right back. "Are you kidding me? You've been wanting to do this all your life and now that it's here, you're asking is it worth it? Anousheh, are you absolutely *crazy?*"

I wasn't crazy. And now I saw the determination in the eyes that stared back at me and I knew, yes, it was worth it, every bit of it. In fact, I was convinced my life would not be complete without going into space because it was my destiny to make this journey. When I returned, I promised myself I would make up for all the hardships I had caused Hamid and everyone else. I would be a fury in our company, doing everything I could to build it up and keep it on track. But at that moment, I was determined to fly as close to the stars as I could get. I had worked too hard and I deserved to go!

I pushed the doom demon off my shoulder and allowed myself to think about the launch and even savor it a little. More than anything, I looked forward to getting up there and floating free of all the fears, anxieties, and expectations of the world. I tried to imagine myself weightless and, for a moment, felt free and joyful. But then, I found myself once more filled with misgivings. I could actually feel the pressure of the air I was breathing and it was like a huge weight on my chest. The demon had crawled back up on my shoulder again, whispering at me to be afraid.

Go away! That was my message to that demon and everyone else who might be out there trying to stop me. *Whether you like it or not, I am going into space where there will be no more doctors, no more cold stethoscopes, no more ceremonies, and no more negativity from people who like to cause consternation and pain.* Now I understood why, moments before the 1961 launch of the first American manned spaceflight, Alan Shepard so furiously demanded, "I'm cooler than you are . . . light this candle!" I understood why Yuri Gagarin kept urging the technicians to keep working during his countdown, saying, "Feeling fine, excellent spirits; let's go!" then a jubilant "Off we go!" at launch. I was in the same mode. *Strap me in, slam shut the hatch, and screw down the bolts, gentlemen. It is time for Anousheh Ansari to leave the earth. So let's get on with it!*

My family was coming to see me that afternoon and I could not wait to see their faces and hear their voices. Of course, since we were still in quarantine, we'd only be able to talk to each other through glass. This would be my only chance to see to them before my flight, my only chance to tell Hamid again how much I loved him and appreciated what he had done for me, my only chance to joke around with Amir, my only chance to console my mom and tell her I would be back before she knew it, and to tell Atousa not to worry and to be strong for both of us. But what words would form to let me do all that? Was it even possible?

I did my morning exercises, first on a stationary bike in the tiny workout room, and then a quick run around the compound. The fresh air worked its wonders and I came back from my run feeling great. I showered, followed with a few last reviews of some launch procedures, and then I had the rest of the day free until my family visit. The time for the visit came and went but nobody showed up to escort me. I kept looking at my huge watch. There wasn't much time left for the visit. I paced around the room. Each minute was like an hour. *What's going on? Has the launch been scrubbed? Have I been scrubbed? Where is my escort?*

Finally! A knock on my door and a voice telling me it was time to go down to the visitor's room. Relieved, I quickly padded my way down the stairs to a room divided by a glass wall. To my delight, I saw my father, his hair white as snow. He smiled when he saw me. Our eyes met and, at that moment, I saw the love I had longed to see since I was a child. It seemed to pour out of him straight into my heart. I wanted to tell him I had always loved him and how happy I was he had come so far to support me, knowing especially how difficult the long journey was with his physical ailments.

I saw my wonderful, always faithful mother choking back her tears. Atousa wasn't holding anything back. Tears were streaming down her face and I joined her, sobbing openly. Then everyone in the room was either crying or swallowing hard. Atousa retreated to a corner in the back of the room and her husband, Kasra, went along to console her. Tears trickling down my face, I kept smiling and signing with my hands for everyone to come forward and get closer to me. Atousa would later tell me that seeing me behind that glass wall made everyone feel like they were visiting an inmate on death row!

More beloved faces began to register through my teary eyes. My brother-in-law Jamshid was there with his wife, Fariba, and their lovely daughters, Beeta and Tara, their sweet smiles lighting up the room. Aunt Chamsi was there, wearing a Russian fur hat and looking for all the world like a beautiful model. Her smile warmed me inside and out and I could almost see Uncle Frank standing there beside her, so proud of me. He *was* there, of course, as was my Buhbuh with his lighted cane and his dapper suit, saying, *You were my greatest gift in life, Anousheh.* Oh, Buhbuh, without you, I would be nothing!

My cousin Afshin was there and I was so glad to see him. And there was Hamid's father, my sweet Baba Joon, and his wife Debbie. My journey had brought my family together. They smiled and waved, although I saw a certain amount of trepidation in Baba Joon's eyes. I knew he was trying to act strong as the elder of the family and be a rock for everyone else. I had to laugh when I saw Amir so focused on videoing the whole event, and of course, there was my beloved Hamid doing his best to keep things organized. As I pushed myself through that glass wall into his dark eyes, it was as if someone reached up inside me and toggled a switch. All my worries vanished. Such is his strength to me.

I had to talk through an old-fashioned desk microphone, which made me feel a bit like a stand-up comedian, but I clearly wasn't very funny, since there were so few smiles. I asked, "Why are you all being so quiet?" and then everybody began to talk at once. Through the jumble of voices, I heard Papa tell me my grandmother was too ill to travel. It was a reminder that everything, even at that moment, was not all about me. Like everyone in my family, I was worried about Maman but I also knew there were few women in the world with such an indomitable spirit.

Amir had the idea of a family photograph and after some maneuvering we managed to get everyone lined up with me in the middle. The result was a photograph of all of us on both sides of the family that I will cherish forever. There may have been a glass wall between us, but, in my heart, I still held every hand and kissed every cheek.

The Russians tapped on their watches, nodding toward the exit door. I said my goodbyes, my eyes lingering on Hamid, and was escorted into another room to see a movie titled "White Sun of the Desert." I would rather have spent more time with my family, but this was part of the complex ritual the Russians go through before spaceflight. Yuri Gagarin had watched this film the night before his record-breaking orbit, so we would, too. The movie was about a Russian soldier somewhere in a desert country during the Communist revolution who got captured by rebel warriors. Pretty soon, he was with a harem of pretty women and being chased by everybody. Surprising myself, I actually found the movie entertaining. Afterward, there was another physical exam, another dinner, and finally lights out. I was told someone would come for me at one in the morning. The doctor gave me a pill to help me sleep. Fearful I would oversleep, I took only half of it.

I was just settling down when there came a rap on my bedroom door. I opened it and saw it was none other than Doctor Morose from my centrifuge test. Instantly, that demon jumped up on my shoulder and prodded me with his pitchfork! I worried I had failed something and I was going nowhere but home, just like poor Dice-K! But the doctor only smiled and apologized for disturbing me, then handed me an envelope and left. In the envelope was a DVD from my family that Amir had orchestrated. I watched it, crying and laughing at the same time. It contained messages of love from my family. When Amir came on, he made me promise I would return safe and sound because he couldn't handle Hamid without me. That one earned a knowing chuckle.

The half of the sleeping pill was kicking in, and I felt my eyelids grow heavy. I shut down my laptop and checked my alarm for the hundredth time, then slipped beneath the covers of my hard little bed. I wondered about the rocket that would carry me into space. Was the propellant being pumped inside it at that moment? I should have known such things, but there was always so much to learn, so much to understand, and so many people telling me things in three different languages.

I tried to remember what I knew of the *Soyuz* rocket. It is not huge like NASA's space shuttle or anything like the massive *Saturns* the Americans built to go to the moon, but it is probably the most reliable rocket in the world. I was told the *Soyuzes* had been launched nearly 900 times, far more than any other space booster. The first one had lifted off back in 1966 and the series was actually based on an even older design from the 1950s. Soyuz rockets were, in effect, human-carrying intercontinental ballistic missiles built by the Soviet Union to launch nuclear weapons. Thank God they were never used for that purpose.

Despite their reliable reputation, the technology was old and I knew that *Soyuz* rockets had failed recently. In October 2002, an uncrewed variant had faltered 29 seconds into its launch, falling back to Earth and exploding on the ground. One person was killed and eight others were injured. In June 2005, the third stage of a *Soyuz* carrying a military communications satellite failed to ignite. The payload crashed into Siberia. What would have happened if there had been a crew aboard? Russian spacecraft have escape towers to blast crew capsules away from exploding or failing boosters, but those are designed to work at low altitudes. A failure of the upper stages would find the crew miles above the earth, the escape tower long since ejected. All the contingency plans in that case were basically untested.

And then there was *Soyuz 11.* Carrying three cosmonauts in 1971 to a *Salyut* space station, the mission had set a new space-endurance record. When the cosmonauts landed in their heat-scarred spacecraft, the Russian recovery crew raced to open the hatch and congratulate the three men inside. They found them, still strapped into their seats, all dead from asphyxiation. A simple valve, designed to equalize pressure, had jolted open during the separation phase of the habitation and descent modules. It is not always the big things that kill you in spaceflight. Rather, it's often the little things that go unnoticed, like that little valve aboard the *Soyuz 11,* or the rubber O-ring on the *Challenger's* solid rocket boosters, made too stiff by an unexpected cold snap in Florida.

But at that moment, past failures didn't matter. I had told many people I was willing to die for my dream of venturing into space. *Do your worst, rocket,* I thought. *Turn my body into kerosene-stained atoms if you can. I'm going to ride you as high as you'll take me.* A Zen-like feeling descended over me. I was ready to fly or die.

My official cosmonaut watch beeped. The time had come for me to go into space. I rose and looked again at my reflection in the window. I was grinning madly.

I took my last shower, braided my hair in twin pigtails, and put on my official training coveralls. When the knock came to wake me, I was ready to go, and I hurried out into the hall and down the stairs to the breakfast room. Misha and L. A. were already there. I said good morning in a soft voice and quietly ate my breakfast. Dr. Shannan Moynihan, the American flight surgeon who had befriended me during training at Star City and was now my official surgeon, arrived and escorted me back to my room. She carried with her an old metal basin with medical gauze soaked in alcohol. The Russians required that she take a culture from every part of my body. She also had to make certain I wiped myself all over with the alcohol-drenched gauze. She took the samples one by one and I wiped myself down, shivering as the alcohol evaporated off my exposed skin. It seemed to me that any cultures taken from my skin wouldn't be anything unusual and the alcohol wipe-down couldn't possibly kill enough bacteria to make a difference. In the hours I was about to spend inside a hot spacesuit, I was certain many more would grow. But once again, I did what I had to do to keep the doctors happy. I suspected the alcohol wipe-down was another Russian ritual, something Yuri Gagarin had done, so we would do it too.

While I stood there, nearly naked and shivering, a Russian nurse arrived and Shannan handed her the kit to take away. Then she gave me a set of white long johns. We had spoken little during the wipe-down. Now she asked, "Are you doing OK?"

"Great," I answered and said nothing more. I didn't want to jinx anything.

I climbed into the long underwear, then my training suit. I had just zipped them up when Peggy Whitson came by to say goodbye. I saw she was carrying a satellite phone and I asked if I could use it to call my grandmother. Maman answered and I told her where I was and what I was about to do. She replied that she was proud of me, then wished me good luck and a safe return. Her voice was weak but I knew she was the same old Maman. She ordered me to come back soon and then come to see her. I told her to start counting down because I would see her in two weeks. I thanked Peggy and gave her the phone back. She had been wonderful to me all along. I was disappointed that I would not get the chance to fly with her.

I then had to autograph my apartment door—another Yuri Gagarin tradition. My signature went next to those of my friends Marcos Pontes and Greg Olsen, the third Space Adventures flyer. After going back downstairs to meet up with Misha and L. A., we attended a brief prayer session given by a black-frocked Orthodox priest. The Russians had asked me if I had any objection to participating in a Christian ceremony, and I replied that a prayer in any language and any religion is still a prayer and I welcomed it. We stood in front of the priest and he recited a prayer for our safe return. Misha made the sign of the cross and then the priest shook holy water in our faces. L. A. looked a bit startled by the face spray and managed a small, embarrassed smile. We moved on to a farewell gathering with the senior members of our support team. I did my best not to look at my watch during the ceremonial speeches. Time itself seemed to be bogged down.

At our waiting bus, family, friends, and journalists lined the pavement, snapping pictures and shooting video. Mom was crying, and I felt a little bad because I was so happy. I tried to wipe the smile from my face but it kept coming back. Once on the bus, I waved and blew kisses. Hamid's face was etched with concern. I mouthed to him, "Don't worry, everything is going to be fine."

The bus headed to the building where we would don our Sokol launch-and-reentry suits. As the bus rumbled on, Misha, L. A., and I became very quiet. Then the Russians announced they had a surprise for us. They turned on a small television mounted to the ceiling, and there was L. A.'s wife and son telling him how much they loved him and to be safe. L. A.'s face brightened. Then Misha's family greeted him and sent him their love. Next came my surprise: a message from Hamid, the first part in Farsi telling me how everyone was probably wondering what he was saying and how puzzled they must be. I laughed at his little joke and then became serious as he told me how much he loved me, that millions of people had their eyes to the sky praying for my safe return, and that he would be waiting for me with open arms. He signed off, saying he would speak to me in space.

We arrived at a hangar-like building to complete our final preparations. We sat on plastic chairs for more than an hour, discussing why we'd gotten up so early only to wait. The only explanation was that it must be another Gagarin ritual. Peggy and Yuri came by. Since they were our official backups, I suppose they could have taken our places if we were sick. But had I been bitten by a cobra that morning, or fallen down steps and broken my leg, I would have said I was in perfect health.

Some technicians arrived with another new set of underwear for us, a surprise since I'd only worn mine for a few hours. Misha entered a small dressing room to don his new underwear, then L. A., and then me. My lofty thoughts at that moment were focused on my last chance to go to the bathroom and pee. I was wearing a maximum absorbency garment, which is essentially an adult diaper. From what I had heard, women especially have a hard time urinating in the knees-up position required in the *Soyuz*. I wasn't sure which would be worse: feeling like my bladder was about to explode or sitting for hours in a wet diaper. Desiring neither, I slipped into the bathroom to purge every last molecule of liquid remaining in my bladder.

Wearing a new diaper, new underwear, and adding an EKG harness, I was sent to sit in a chair to wait for my Sokol suit. Officials clustered around us, some snapping photos, some making conversation with one another, and others simply watching us with grave expressions. Then, one by one, we submitted ourselves to the suit techs. When L. A. got into his suit, he sat down and I saw his left leg vibrating. *Aha,* I thought. *A kindred spirit.* Mine was doing the same thing—not out of anxiety, but simply because things were going too slow. Misha, of course, was solid as a rock. He sat there with his hands on his knees, looking pleasant and calm, as if going into space was an everyday occurrence.

I stepped into my suit as I had practiced many times and, with the help of the suit tech, pulled it over my head and poked my head through the neck ring. One advantage of being small is that it made getting into the suit less difficult. Afterward, we sat for photographs and then trudged with as much grace as possible into a room with a glass wall. There we waited for final approval from the officials and a leak check of our suits.

On the other side of the glass wall, seated in the front row, was my family, Misha's family, L. A.'s family, and a gaggle of officials and reporters. My family pressed in close. Hadn't we already played out this scene? I was once more reminded of the film *Groundhog Day* where everything happened the same way again and again. Still, it was great to see everyone and I waved and made hand signals that all was well.

For the leak check, we climbed into mock-ups of our seats. We sat on our backs with our knees practically to our chins. The check accomplished, we were pulled up and told we were good to go. Officials crowded around for handshakes and I thought to myself, *Well, that's going to add to the bacteria count!*

At our final press conference, most of the reporters' questions were for me, and I felt bad because Misha and L. A. got so few. I was asked, inevitably, about the patch problem ("No problem," was my answer); how the crew was treating me ("Great!"); and the situation between Iran and the United States ("I am not a politician.").

We were then escorted to an empty room for a few welcome moments of privacy and peace. To protect the footpads of our Sokol suits, we put on heavy gray boots and, to keep us cool, were connected to little suitcaselike ventilators.

Finally, we received the signal that it was time to go, and exited the building to the music of a Russian march. People applauded and cheered as we walked to some white squares marked on the asphalt. Russian officials saluted and Misha and L. A. saluted back. It was still dark and the camera flashes were blinding. After a few short speeches, we plodded to the bus, waving at everyone. I searched the crowd until I spotted Atousa and Mom. They were both crying and the way their lips were moving, I knew they were saying prayers. I still couldn't wipe the smile off my face.

Once I was seated on the bus, I saw that Mom had somehow broken free and was banging with both hands on my window. I tried to calm her down by sending her air kisses. When the bus began to move, she ran after it. Thank goodness Hamid saw her and quickly came over to calm her down. I sat back in my seat, trying to absorb everything.

The next tradition, which I thought was funny, was for the boys to get out of the bus and pee on the tires. This also started with Gagarin, who must have forgotten to go earlier. Fortunately, I was excused from this particular exercise, although I asked Misha to think of me when he was doing his business so I would at least be participating mentally. He laughed and said, "Sure, Anousheh."

While the boys were being boys, I grew impatient. I thought the Russians were nice and their rituals added a special touch to the whole experience, but I just needed to get into space. I looked down and saw my leg vibrating like a tuning fork. *Come on, guys! Make water and get it over with!*

Finally, the men got back on board, their duty accomplished, and our bus crept closer to the rocket. There were cloudy vapors of liquid oxygen venting from it like a white-hot teakettle except, in this case, the teakettle was supercold. Oxygen can only be liquid if it's cooled to minus 297 degrees Fahrenheit. When LOX, as it is known in the space business, is combined with kerosene, there is a huge release of energy, and hot gases flow like supersonic rivers through bell-like nozzles. Newton's third law is rigidly enforced: for every action, there is an equal and opposite reaction.

We stopped at the base of the rocket and climbed the near-vertical ladder leading to a tiny elevator barely big enough for the three of us. We waved at the small, cheering crowd and then crammed ourselves in with a couple of the ground crew. Up we went on a slow ride to the top. It felt like popping out of a sardine can when the elevator door finally opened. A platform covered with protective canvas led to the habitation module and its beckoning hatch. I climbed in without any hesitation.

After entering the hab module, the written procedure required me to lower myself through a hatch into the descent module, then move to my assigned seat on the right. To prepare for this maneuver, I had done dips every day, building up my arms. There is a tiny step that can be unfolded to help, but I was too short to reach it. During practice runs, I had nearly always missed the step and fallen feet first onto the commander's seat. Fearing I might damage my suit, the hatch, the seat, or myself, the Russians opted to put someone inside the capsule to help me. I didn't argue when I heard about their plan.

I had to descend backwards through the hatch to avoid scratching my helmet's faceplate on the lid. As I lowered myself, my helper formed a step with his hand and I murmured my thanks. The capsule seemed much smaller, probably because of all the extra things, such as outdoor survival gear, packed inside. After stepping off my helper's makeshift step, I carefully placed my boots on the commander's chair and slowly turned around and stepped across onto my seat. My helper handed me the ventilation and oxygen hoses. Without a flow of air in the suit, sweat was rolling down my face. I lowered myself into my seat, careful first to smooth out any folds in the bottom of my suit. This was something Marcos had taught me. Although launch was supposed to occur only an hour or two after we were sealed inside the capsule, it might be longer and I didn't want a wad of material bunched up under my behind.

Once I was in position I started fastening my belts, and in the few seconds I was alone, took note of a small stuffed bear hanging in front of the middle seat on a string. I knew its story. Cosmonaut commanders have permission to hang a small personal object in the capsule. Misha had chosen a little bear his daughter had given him. "Misha" is also a favorite nickname for bear toys in Russia.

L. A.'s long legs came dangling through the hatch. He stood on the commander's chair and slowly turned around to lower himself into the left seat. There were beads of sweat on his forehead. His helmet barely fit between the hatch and the rescue packages installed on the wall. Wanting to be helpful, I pushed the hatch back so he could move into his seat. He finally managed to get seated and started to hook himself up, asking me to turn on the ventilation switch located on my side. We both felt the air blowing inside our spacesuits to cool us down. After a few moments, he turned to me and said, "How are you?"

I smiled and said, "Everything is great!" Little did he know, a fire could have been raging under my rump and I would have probably said the same thing. A few minutes later, Misha climbed inside the capsule, his face also covered with droplets of sweat. He pointed at the bear and chuckled.

We were still about two hours away from launch, and there were a series of procedures for Misha and L. A. to go through while the technicians on the ground also did their final checks. I was responsible for only a few things: to turn on the condensation valve between the habitation module and descent module when told to do so, to open the suit ventilation valve as needed (already accomplished), to engage the emergency oxygen valve if so instructed by the commander and, if requested, to hand over the extra flight data files situated next to me. However trivial, I was determined to accomplish my tasks perfectly. Misha and L. A. combed through their procedures packets while I made some personal notes on the margins of mine, trying to capture my thoughts prior to launch. I felt quite calm.

The next two hours swept by. There was another suit-pressure check and a hatch-leak check. The three of us had to coordinate these tasks precisely and make sure we didn't miss the calls for each pressure reading. If there was any kind of anomaly, we would have only one more chance to do it correctly, or the launch would be scrubbed. I had worried about this but wound up doing fine, and after our final reading, Misha announced we were ready for flight. To my surprise, I heard the sound of soft classical music playing in my headset. Just as I was starting to enjoy the music, I felt the rocket stirring to life. Misha put out his gloved hands and L. A. put his on top of them. I wasn't going to be left out, so I put my hands on top of theirs. As we sat back, Misha said, "Ready . . . here we go!"

In my earphones, I heard the count in Russian.

"Nine . . . eight . . . seven . . ."

It was really happening! *Thank you, God. Thank you for helping me realize my dream.* I felt the little girl inside me giggle and thought my heart might explode from joy.

"Six . . . five . . . four . . ."

I'm really going . . .

"Three . . ."

I love you, Hamid!

"Two . . ."

"One."

Ooooooomth!

A great wave of energy was released below and I felt an incredibly powerful shove. When, some months ago, I had watched a *Soyuz* blast off with all its thunder, I never imagined it would be this smooth during ascent. It was like a jet airplane taking off on a short runway. As we climbed, I felt the Gs press me down, but they were mild. I glanced at the stuffed bear. Its string was taut and quivering.

As we rose, the protective cover over our capsule was ejected with a jarring thud and rays of light flooded inside. Time had shrunk to nothing. There was a shudder that announced the separation of the final rocket stage. I looked to my left and saw Misha the bear drifting peacefully, its string formed into relaxed curves. The sight of it made me laugh. At last! I was free of the earth.

I felt myself lift slightly off the seat. I could hardly believe it wasn't all just a dream. What did it look like outside? I wanted to press my face against the porthole but was strapped in so tightly I couldn't move. We were in orbit but there was one last check, the test of an antenna needed to navigate and dock our capsule to the space station. A green light was supposed to come on within six minutes to indicate that this antenna was functioning properly. Misha watched the timer as I held my breath. If that light didn't come on, it meant we couldn't dock and would have to descend to Earth. I kept my eyes fixed on the timer and waited for that light to go green. After the rush of takeoff, every second felt like an hour. When the digital timer reached zero, there was no green light. There was dead silence in the capsule, our eyes riveted on that little light. I wanted to bang on it to see if it was burnt out or maybe loose. My hopes and dreams were about to be shattered because of that little thing! Then it happened. The little light turned green. I let out a sigh of pure delight, and knew without a doubt at that moment that I was going to the International Space Station.

A few moments later, Misha said it was OK to open our visors and loosen our belts. L. A. took off a glove and it floated through the cabin. This made me laugh again. I wondered what these two space professionals thought of me, this giggling schoolgirl they'd carried along. Throwing off my belts, I was able to take a look through the tiny porthole of the capsule and saw Earth from space for the first time. My laughter stopped as tears welled in my eyes. I saw a small crystal float away from me. It was beautiful, a pretty little diamond. I wondered where it came from, if perhaps some worker had lost the stone from her ring. Then I realized it was one of my tears. It seemed to be attracted to the earth. It touched the glass in the porthole and became for just a moment the tiniest of rainbows. I could not catch my breath. My beautiful planet, under the warm rays of the sun, turned gracefully beneath me. I was entranced.

While I watched in silent rapture, Misha and L. A. lifted out of their seats and rose into the habitation module to prepare our spacecraft for life in orbit. After a short while, Misha pushed his head through the hatch and told me I could change. It took a moment to process why he was upside down, at least from my perspective. He reached behind the seats and handed me a pair of woolen overalls and a jacket. I opened all the bands, zippers, and hooks of my spacesuit and slipped it off. Everything was suddenly so easy in zero-G.

After I got into my coveralls, Misha and I reattached the gloves to our suits and positioned them in our seats so that the ventilation hoses could dry them out. They looked so funny. With their visors closed you couldn't tell if someone was in them or not. Misha said we could hide and let the mission control folks think we were in our seats. Of course, we couldn't go very far.

I thought I would try my hand at flying and stood up on the middle seat, pushing against it. I floated through the hatch into the hab module. I thought I was doing pretty well until I realized I didn't have any brakes. I kept on floating, giggling all the while, until I bumped my head on the docking hatch.

Now the trick was figuring out how to get back. I pushed my hand against the wall, more gently this time, but went sailing out of control. I bounced off the base of the hab module and pushed off again before grabbing a handle on the side, thinking it would stop me. Instead, it created a sort of rotational momentum, and while my upper body stayed in place, my legs continued on their journey.

L. A. was trying to prepare the food station, but I could tell he was also watching me out of the corner of his eye. He smiled indulgently. I suppose for him it was like seeing a child trying to take her first steps. I didn't care. I was determined to learn how to fly. Finally, he grabbed my arm and lowered me down to some foot straps on the deck. I slipped my feet under them to see what he wanted. Silently, he handed me a food pack of cookies and crackers, along with canned meat, vegetables, and sweets. Didn't he know I wasn't interested in food? I was in space! I peered through the porthole to see where I was. We were soaring over the Pacific Ocean, approaching Mexico. The blue of the ocean was so gorgeous, it left me speechless.

To satisfy L. A., I ate, but figured I should keep it light for the first day. I opened up some crackers and washed them down with apple juice sucked through a straw from a paper carton. When I swallowed, I wondered what was happening to the food in my stomach. I worried the apple juice would float up into my throat, but everything seemed fine. It's odd. Have our bodies been especially designed to work in zero gravity? It was the first of many philosophical questions I pondered in space.

Misha and L. A. asked me if I was having fun. I knew what they were really asking was whether I felt sick. I was pleased to announce that I was fine. In fact, I was better than fine—I had clearly been born to live in space. I kept looking through the porthole as we soared around the world. Actually, we were slowly tumbling end over end. This is because when the combined *Soyuz* habitation and descent modules are put into orbit, the attached solar panels must face the sun. Since the panels are positioned like wings on an airplane, the module combo can't stabilize itself by spinning like a bullet— if it did, the solar arrays would be constantly moving in and out of the sunlight. Instead, to maintain the correct orientation, the *Soyuz* must gradually rotate around its horizontal axis. The trip to the station was going to take close to two days, which is a long time to be going tailbone-over-teakettle at five miles a second. I finally understood why we had been put in that dreaded spinning chair. The Russian trainers had told me not to look outside the first day because it would make me sick, but I just couldn't resist.

I ate more crackers and cookies for dinner and then it was bedtime. Our sleep cycle had been shifted back to prepare us for the clock aboard the International Space Station, but we were all so tired that going to sleep early was no problem. Misha retreated into the descent module to sleep. Marcos had advised me that to avoid space sickness, I should hang my sleeping bag from the ceiling of the hab module. That way my head would be closer to the center of mass and get less of the tumbling effect. I followed his directions and slipped into my bag. L. A. hung his bag from the ceiling across from me. We looked like bats in a tiny cave.

Just to be safe, I decided to take a motion-sickness pill. I put on my iPod headphones and snuggled into my bat sack, a happy space camper. It felt strange, but I loved it. I could just imagine how popular a hotel in space would be. I could hear the pitch now: *Step right up, ladies and gentlemen!*

Go into space and sleep on the ultimate bed made of nothing but molecules of air. I imagine this would be the ultimate honeymoon suite!

Falling asleep in zero-G: I thought maybe I should pinch myself just in case this really was a dream. But no, it was too vivid, too beautiful to be a dream. When my eyes opened the next morning, I slipped out of my bag and flew headfirst into the capsule, then flipped around and flew right back up. As soon as I stopped, I realized this was not a good idea. It seemed that while I slept, space monsters had invaded our ship. One of them had crawled up inside me and squeezed all the blood from my shriveled body into my skull, which felt like a balloon about to pop. Yet another monster had grabbed my spine with both hands and wrenched it apart until every nerve was screaming in horrible pain. Some kind of creature was also doing a cha-cha inside my belly. The crackers and cookies and some of the breakfast I'd had the day before announced they were on their way up to see me.

I was a woman of space.

I was also sick as a dying dog.

At Home among the Stars

I spent the day feeling awful. After consulting with the doctors on the ground, Misha gave me an injection of anti-nausea medicine, which didn't make me feel much better but at least allowed me to sleep. I moved my sleeping bag in the hab module between two large green containers. Curling up into a fetal position inside the bag, I was able to press the top of my head against one of them, my feet against the other, and my back pressed against the wall. This awkward posture oddly gave me some relief. But the next morning, I woke up and still felt rotten. This made me angry, so I asked for another injection. Misha got permission to give it to me and I watched as he delicately pushed the needle into my arm. I kept apologizing. Here I had thought I was born for space, but now I felt deathly ill. I kept telling myself: *Anousheh, stop this nonsense! You are stronger than this. Get hold of yourself. This is all in your head and you can stop it!*

But I couldn't stop it. I just wasn't functioning. After a while, I decided that if I could only get to the International Space Station, everything would be better. When I voiced this opinion, both L. A. and Misha told me I was wrong, that going from a small volume to a larger one would probably make me even sicker. But I didn't care what they said. I was convinced I needed to get out of that little gray-green can and inside the station.

When I woke up the next time, I was feeling better. Cautiously, I slipped out of my sleeping bag and started to slowly move around. My throat was dry so I drank a little apple juice. My sickness had caused me to lose a day and half in space and I wasn't happy about it. Misha flew into the hab module to tell me there were only a few hours to go before we reached the station. He went on to say he was sorry but I would have to get into my Sokol suit. Taking it easy, I climbed into the suit while Misha and L. A. prepared us to dock. Misha called out to me, "Anousheh you must be seated *now!*" I picked up the pace, hooking the last hook and tightening the last belt of the suit and entered the *Soyuz* capsule, flying over Misha's head. I twisted myself into my seat and put on my safety belts. Misha reached over and tugged on them to make sure they were nice and tight.

The docking process took a long time. In front of me, there was a tiny screen used to track our approach. When I spotted the tiny dot that represented the station on the screen, it was like seeing the first sign of light at the end of a dark tunnel. We moved steadily toward it and it kept growing bigger and bigger. Finally, there it was, a vast, glittering island in the sky. I was reminded of a quote from *The Little Prince:* "What makes the desert beautiful," said the little prince, "is that somewhere it hides a well." Now I understood what that boy from the stars meant. At that moment, what made space beautiful was that somewhere it hid a refuge and we had found it.

It felt like we were going very slow but as we got closer, I thought we were going too fast. I realized my right foot was pressing down as if I were putting on the brakes of a skidding car. Fortunately, Misha had everything under control and we docked smoothly, the probe on the *Soyuz* gently clicking into place. We were attached to the space station like a remora on a giant whale.

Nothing seems to happen very fast in space, which is strange because we were actually going five miles a second. Before we could open the hatch, we had to go through dozens of checks. Misha said we could get out of our space suits and into our coveralls. I did, and happily discovered I was hungry. I ate a few crackers and decided to freshen up. I knew there would be cameras pointed at us when we entered the station, and I didn't want to look like a pale, sick, pitiful thing. I rooted around until I found my personal hygiene kit but when I opened it, I was astonished to find it wasn't mine at all but Dice-K's—razor, shaving cream, and all! I made do with a wet towel and some moisturizer taken from another kit, which also held my lip gloss; my eyeliner; the coin that Marcos had given me for luck; and a special necklace holding my wedding ring, Uncle Frank's wedding ring, and a ring that belonged to my Buhbuh. With my X Prize hat on and my special necklace around my neck, I was prepared for my close-up.

Finally the hatch was ready to be opened. Misha and L. A. called me over and told me to be prepared to "smell space." Like a good little space cadet, I positioned myself to inhale deeply when the hatch was opened. When it was, I detected a strange odor I described as being "sort of like burnt almond cookies." Both of my crewmates looked at me like I was crazy.

By this time, our greeting party—station commander Pavel Vinogradov, flight engineer Jeff Williams, and European Space Agency astronaut Thomas Reiter—were ready for us. When they opened the ISS hatch, L. A., Misha, and I flew inside the station. I took a look around at the racks of experiments, ventilation tubes, and whirring fans, and instantly felt at home. Pavel, who invited me to call him Pasha, was a typically hearty Russian cosmonaut, filled with good cheer and verve. Jeff, a crisp, disciplined colonel in the United States Army, was more reserved, but I liked him from the first. I already knew Thomas from Star City. We had shared a table for several breakfasts in the Prophy kitchen. He gave me a friendly smile of recognition.

After a few minutes, I was told that the ground crew had gathered our friends and family to speak to us. We positioned ourselves in front of a television camera and a microphone on a cord was handed to each of us in turn. Although we couldn't see the people on the ground, they could see us. When his turn came to speak, Hamid wanted to know how I felt and I told him everything was OK. He answered, "I was worried. They said you were sick!"

I laughed it off and told him it was nothing serious, just motion sickness and I was really fine. With my answer, I could hear the relief in his voice. He added we would have our first daily private call in the morning. There was so much more he wanted to tell me, but only in private. I replied with a smile and a blown kiss, saying, "I can't wait!" Then the satellite pass was completed and our communications shut down.

While L. A., Misha, and Thomas talked business, Pasha volunteered to give me a quick tour. I followed him like a lost puppy, my eyes wide as saucers. I was getting my "space legs" but still preferred to pull myself along using the handles spaced throughout the station, instead of the leisurely free flight of the pros. (Mainly, I didn't want to make a fool of myself in front of Pasha by banging my head on something.) As we moved through the station, he pointed out the various nooks where I could place my sleeping bag. I considered them all but then saw the place I wanted most of all because of the privacy it afforded and a big round porthole with an excellent view of the earth. It was in Docking Compartment 1 (DC-1), which is attached to the service module. "But it is so noisy and cold here!" Pasha exclaimed. He gestured toward a fan. "It never stops."

"I don't care," I said, pointing at a porthole. "I want to be able to look out and watch the world and stars go by."

Pasha did a zero-G Russian shrug and said, "It's up to you," then showed me how to install a curtain so I could have some privacy. "When you put this up, no one will bother you," he said. He also took a moment to show me the best way to take photographs through the window, explaining I needed to compensate for glare and to use the manual mode so I could zoom in on the subject. He also cautioned me about hitting the window with the camera or anything else, saying it already had a lot of scratches on it and it couldn't be replaced. Then he surprised me with an album of photographs he'd downloaded from his camera onto the Russian laptop. "I heard you wanted photos of Iran, Texas, and some other places," he said. "So I thought I would help. Here are the ones I took."

The photos were wonderful. They included Mashhad, my birthplace; Tehran, where I'd grown up; northern Virginia, where I'd first come to the United States and gone to college; Plano, Texas, where I had been successful in business; and the big island of Hawaii, the site of the Mauna Kea observatory. He also included some beautiful pictures of the full moon, knowing that I would not be able to observe a full moon during my stay. I was so touched by Pasha's thoughtfulness, I wanted to hug him. I settled for a heartfelt "*Spasibo!*" which is Russian for "Thank you!" He seemed so different from the serious man I had a met a few times in Star City. He was so at ease in space.

The ISS at that time consisted of the *Zarya* control module (or FGB) assembly, the *Unity* node, the *Zvezda* service module, the U.S. lab module called *Destiny,* some multipurpose logistic modules, the Canadian robot arm, and assorted trusses, mating adapters, airlocks, and solar panels. Although it was only about a third of the size it was going to be when completed, the ISS was still huge compared to the tiny *Soyuz.* It was like being inside a series of connected trailers filled with interesting scientific and communications equipment. I was dazzled and intrigued by everything I saw and already wanted to stay much longer than the week planned. I was jealous of the professionals aboard. Did they realize how truly blessed they were? It seemed to me sometimes they had a sort of casual acceptance of their situation, whereas I was so thankful just to be there. I decided to make every second count.

✺

Just before we arrived, the NASA space shuttle *Atlantis* had detached with a six-person crew, heading home. We watched their takeoff on television while we were in quarantine. I heard from Jeff that they were a pretty happy bunch, having successfully completed three EVAs (extravehicular activities, popularly known as spacewalks) to install their cargo of trusses and solar arrays.

"Anousheh, come see *Atlantis*," L. A. called a few hours after we were aboard the station. I headed toward the view port where he was peering outside. He was watching the shuttle. "They're just hitting the atmosphere," he said. This reminded me of *Columbia's* fate and I began to worry.

I saw a flash of orange color that turned very bright with a streak of white tail. It looked like a beautiful slow motion comet. At a loss for words, I managed an awed "Wow!"

L. A. said, "They'll be on the runway in fifteen minutes." He sounded envious. Me? I was glad I wasn't with them. I liked right where I was. Of course, I didn't have more than 200 days of low-earth orbit in front of me as L. A. did.

In the hours that followed, I settled into my new home. Marcos had left a video camera on board with permission for me to use it. I looked around until I found it and starting making a home movie. I also had a Nikon camera with me. It was the same type that Dice-K had planned to take and had therefore been approved. Peggy had advised me that it was always best to take fresh cameras into space because radiation was so rough on them.

Although I enjoyed poking around and taking pictures, I looked forward to the first sleep period, since I would be bedding down with beautiful Earth as my companion. Our planet did not disappoint. I all but pressed my nose against the window and watched the wonderful world with all its colors and textures rolling below. I could see the curvature of the earth and the atmosphere above it, so thin yet so necessary for life. The bands of the air were bluish in color, each getting darker until they disappeared into the blackness of space. As we slipped toward the edge of night, which the astronauts call the terminator, the swirling clouds turned from a fluffy white to the translucent pink of cotton candy. The sun seemed to me to get brighter as the edge of the planet lit up the atmosphere with a hot rainbow of colors before falling into darkness. Once across the terminator, I saw flashes of light below that were not cities, but great thunderstorms tearing through the sky. Then . . . *there!* I was so excited when a city floated into view, its lights radiating outward like a wispy spiderweb. As suddenly as it had appeared, it was gone. I wondered which city it was, or even which hemisphere. I could have gotten up and checked the computer that kept track of where we were, but I didn't. I was too content to move.

I'm not certain I ever actually slept that night. I kept watch through my window as long as I could while cities, storms, oceans, continents, islands, and the terminators of day and night swept below me in the most incredible light show ever seen by woman or man.

✦

It takes the International Space Station about 90 minutes to circle the globe and, as a result, there are 16 beautiful sunrises and 16 glorious sunsets over the course of every day, each one different and spectacular in its own way. It would be nice to take note of them all but to avoid psychological burnout, humans require at least a semblance of our usual 24-hour, day and night planetary cycle. The station therefore keeps its clock on Zulu, or Greenwich

Mean Time (GMT) with everything scheduled accordingly, including times to work, eat, and sleep. However, since Moscow mission control's time is three hours behind Greenwich, and the other mission control in Houston six hours ahead, these cycles tend to shift over time, depending on the plan for the day or week. In my case, I went to bed around 7:30 p.m. Zulu with a scheduled wake-up time of 4 a.m. This, of course, presupposed that it was possible for me to actually sleep with all the exciting possibilities of being aboard the station.

On my first morning aboard, I was awake several hours before I was supposed to get up. I relaxed in my sleeping-bag cocoon and marveled at the view. Feeling nature's call, I pushed my curtain aside and got dressed. In my clothing package was a coverall I had forwarded to be stowed aboard and then forgotten about, one that had a red, white, and blue American flag on one side and the pre-Islamic Republic Iranian flag with its bold stripes of red, white, and green on the other. I laughed to myself. After all the controversy about me wearing the colors of the Iranian flag, this coverall had slipped through. I pulled it on and headed to the bathroom, which was next to Thomas Reiter's little cabin. No one else seemed to be up and I felt like a true space explorer as I pulled myself along from handhold to handhold. After taking care of business and thoroughly cleaning myself, I flew back to my window and crawled into my sleeping bag to watch the earth some more.

Pasha was scheduled to help me with my morning call, a PFC, or private family conference, with Hamid. I found him in the service module and said, "*Dobrey Oudra* [Good morning]."

He smiled and said, "*Dobrey Oudra*. Hamid, *da?*" I answered with a great deal of enthusiasm, "*Da!*"

I positioned myself next to the communication panel and put on a big headset. Pasha pointed to his watch and said, "Five minutes." I waited anxiously, thinking of all the questions I had for Hamid. What did my rocket look like when we lifted off? How did Mom and Papa do? How were Amir, Atousa, and Baba Joon? What had he heard from our Prodea employees? As soon as I heard Hamid's voice, I began asking these and other questions in rapid-fire succession. Hamid teased me and made me laugh. He said not to worry, that everything was under control, and that the rest of the family was on their way back home. He went on to inform me that my blog had over a million hits and was growing rapidly. I thought I heard him wrong, but Hamid said, "I'm telling you, it is going to hit five million soon. People are writing to you from all over the world. It is unbelievable!"

I started hearing crackling noises and I knew we were about to lose our connection. I cried, "I miss you! I wish you were here!" and he responded that he *was* there, all I had to do was close my eyes and feel him.

"I love you," I whispered.

"Ditto," he replied and the connection was lost.

I went for my first breakfast on board the station. Meals were in the service module at a foldout table, which happened to be only a few feet from the toilet. I often heard Jeff and Thomas talk about the next space station and how they were going to get involved with the design and make it perfect. Perhaps the toilet/kitchen proximity would be one of the design flaws they would fix.

Making my breakfast required that I add hot water to a pouch of dried oatmeal. It was a procedure that demanded precision. The pouch must first be slipped over a hot-water dispenser, which is in the shape of a cone. Then a series of buttons are pressed to dispense the water. Care had to be taken not to allow even a drop to escape, as the water is extremely hot and even a small bubble of it could scald a person nearby. Determined to avoid trouble, I was careful every time I used it. After allowing the oatmeal to soak for a while in the hot water, I ate with gusto, savoring its texture and taste.

I was joined for breakfast by Pasha, Misha, and Jeff. Pasha asked how my first night had gone, and I told him I had never been happier in my life. "I could just look out my window forever," I said, and then we fell to discussing all the marvels he and the others had seen. They spoke in awe of hurricanes, volcanoes, cities, rain forests, the sea, and the astonishing variety of cloud formations. All agreed we lived on a most lovely planet, too lovely to have to endure all the strife that occurred on it all the time. "Here we are above all that," Pasha said. This was true, but every day, the news still came to us from below; some good, some bad, all very human. We couldn't escape it.

After breakfast, I checked my schedule. I had checked it dozens of times by then but didn't want to miss anything. On the ground, Terri was coordinating everything between Moscow, Houston, and Dallas, a nearly impossible job with all the requests coming in for me to speak while in space to the press, schools, and other organizations. She did a great balancing act, protecting me from some requests so as to give me more free time, and selecting those she knew I would think were important and forwarding them to NASA and the Russians to be approved. She was also in charge of getting approval from NASA for the download of my blog each day.

Pasha helped me install a hard drive on the Russian laptop to store my files, photos, and images. Then it was time to get ready for a video interview with CNN. I scurried back to my "room," found my lip gloss and eyeliner, freshened up, and positioned myself while Pasha set up the video camera in the service module. My debut on American television was with Miles O'Brien. After the interview, I realized I had worn my flag coveralls. Over the course of my time aboard the station, I would wear those same coveralls with the contraband flag on it nearly every time I was televised. The number of complaints? Zero.

My schedule allowed me to spend time taking pictures, so I headed toward my nook and was soon contentedly snapping away at the earth, despite the fact that I couldn't tell what I was looking at without cheating and looking at the computer. From that altitude, all I could see were landmasses separated by bodies of water. I was surprised that there were so few natural landmarks to tell me where I was. The ISS is very Earth-oriented, with most of its view ports facing down, rather than toward deep space. Earth, of course, is the most beautiful view, but I also wanted to spend some time with the stars. During the nighttime passes, I focused on them, trying to pick out constellations. Once more, I wished I could have brought along a telescope, not only for me but for all the amateur astronomers who would never have access to those perfectly clear skies. How wonderful it would be to gaze at the moon, planets, and galaxies with a powerful set of optics! Sometimes, it seems, the big space agencies of the world miss the obvious. When commercial companies build their own space stations, I bet telescopes will be all over the place.

At lunch I opened a food box in the service module and nibbled on some chocolate and cookies, then checked my e-mail and replied to one from Peter Diamandis congratulating me. I wrote back, telling him how important he was to me and that I wouldn't be in space without him.

Next I wrote my first blog post from the station, titled "Hello World," and described my launch aboard the *Soyuz*. It was fun imagining people from all over the world reading my words. As soon as I was done with the blog, I was scheduled to use the IP phone in the U.S. lab to call Peter and the people of the X Prize Foundation. It was so exciting to hear Peter's voice. He said he'd already received my e-mail. We had a fun conversation, and I thanked him and everyone associated with the X Prize again for helping me fulfill my dream.

For dinner, we assembled around the foldout table in the service module and I'm afraid I dominated the conversation with my excited chatter. No one seemed to object. The Russians especially seemed to enjoy the musings of a self-acknowledged space rookie. We had brought with us some fresh vegetables, a special treat for those who'd been aboard for weeks. We had a delightful dinner where I learned that in space it is OK, and indeed required, to play with your food while you eat. When L. A. asked me to pass the bread, I dutifully picked up a miniature loaf and tried to hand it to him. He admonished, "That's not the way you pass things in space. Throw it gently." I took the loaf, slowly pushed it toward him and was delighted to see it move like the Starship *Enterprise* toward him. L. A. caught the bread with his mouth.

After dinner I checked my e-mail again and saw one from Terri that included replies from my first space blog. I was astonished by the number of hits and the hundreds who responded with notes. Most of these messages truly touched my heart:

> Hello Anoushe,
> Very Amazing text, I enjoy your words,
> "The Earth is so beautiful and if we could all see it this way I'm sure we would do everything in our power to preserve it"
> I love you anoushe!!!*

⟢⟁⟁⟣

> Dear Anousheh,
> Your flight is inspiring millions of people around the world. Your path is really shining others path who graduate college and pur-

---

* http://www.anoushehansari.com/blog/092006.php#comment-1920

sue career and then to accomplish such a great task in different way. Believe me a lot's of people very proud of you.

Have a cool time on ISS!!!*

hi to my dearest anoushe
I'm sara,from mashhad
I love you so much
only this
kiss you**

it seems funny, but i see a day when i'm reading a book written by you. about your journey from beginning, from the day you dreamed of space to the day you reached the space. i like to know what it takes to go to space station. last year i didn't even know anousheh ansari but now i can't stop thinking about her. this is just a beginning.***

---

* http://www.anoushehansari.com/blog/092006.php#comment-1921
** http://www.anoushehansari.com/blog/092006.php#comment-1924
*** http://www.anoushehansari.com/blog/092006.php#comment-1946

This is Arash, a medical doctor from Iran. i wish you the best in the space. I hope after getting back from space you(as a representative of iranian people too) will dedicate the message of love and friendship of iranian people to the world despite the ideology of hatred which is being supported and expanded by some guys from inside iran. they are not the real representatives of iranian people in international scenes. you probably can realise who i do mean. Long live.*

Hello dear Mrs. Ansari
I write from Yazd in Iran and I am really happy that I see an Iranian Muslim woman could show the entire world that all Iranian people can be really successful. please, please, please read this and find out that I really love you and all the time think about you and think about me just for a moment.
    A thirteen year old girl from Yazd:
    Sima**

I read the comments again and again, dabbing occasionally at my eyes, as I imagined these kind souls tapping away at their keyboards to contact me. Fi-

---

* http://www.anoushehansari.com/blog/092006.php#comment-1947
** http://www.anoushehansari.com/blog/0930062.php#comment-7357

nally, I closed my mail and made my way through the corridors of the U.S. Lab and the FGB until I reached my nook. I put up my curtain and settled down, my eyes drawn as always to my window. Below, shining blue and white, was the world, filled with so many new and wonderful friends who'd sent me their messages and their love all the way to outer space.

✂◦✺◦✺◦✂

Like everyone, I have my favorite things. My favorite movies include *Star Trek* and all its sequels, *Braveheart, Last of the Mohicans, October Sky, Gladiator, Contact, Pay It Forward,* and *Princess Bride.* Some of my favorite books are *How to Change the World,* by David Bornstein; *The Tipping Point,* by Malcolm Gladwell; *Rocket Boys,* by Homer Hickam; and, of course, *The Little Prince,* or as I knew it in French, *Le Petit Prince,* and in Farsi, *Shazdeh Khouchoulu.* I love popular music like "Faith of the Heart," by Rod Stewart; "Imagine," by John Lennon; "Fragile," by Sting; "Upside Down," by Jack Johnson; "Mass Destruction," by Faithless; "Rise Again," by DJ Sammy; "Fly Me to the Moon," (of course!) by Frank Sinatra; "Zan," by Ziba Shirazi; "Wonderful World," by Louis Armstrong; "Stupid Girls," by Pink; "Stop Your Fussin'," by Toni Childs; and, of course, the wonderful song the Grammy-winning musicians of Deep Dish wrote especially for me, "Be the Change." I also know all the old songs by GooGoosh, a famous Iranian singer, and I think the tango is a lovely dance. I only wish I knew how to do it.

I also have favorite moments in time: looking up at the stars from my grandparents' balcony in Tehran, the day Atousa was born, the moment I first saw Hamid and the day he proposed to me, my birthday celebration that first time atop Mauna Kea, the day the Ansari X Prize was won, the day I began to train as a cosmonaut, and the ride on my rocket into space. There are many others, of course, but these tend to stand out.

Some of my favorite places are Paris, Star City, the Hawaiian island of Kauai, La Cinque Terre on the Italian Riviera, and Yosemite National Park. But I must say my favorite place of all is the International Space Station, and in particular my little nook in the DC-1 airlock attached to the service module. I was in heaven there because I could play my favorite music and think of my favorite times, all the while enjoying the majesty of soaring over the whole earth. Within a day, the space station had become a very dear place to me, a place I savored and never really wanted to leave. If it was not for Hamid and my family, I would have gladly signed up to stay another six months, six years, perhaps the rest of my life. This is how much I loved being in space.

I had always heard the expression "watching the world go by." On the station, the phrase took on an entirely new meaning. As I watched from high above, I saw the earth appear to slowly rotate beneath me in the opposite direction. The reality is that we were both rotating in the same direction, but because the space station is going about twenty times faster, it flashes ahead, producing the illusion of our planet going backwards.

The view was also different depending on which window I looked from. From the big window in the service module, the perspective was nearly straight down, and all I could see was the surface of the planet, no visible curvature at the edges. From the window in my nook, I could see a splendid arc of bright blue and white-swirled Earth against the sparkling background of the universe and galaxies of stars. This view was my favorite.

During periods of sunlight, I saw hundreds of shades of blue in the ocean, depending on how deep it was and how the sun reflected off its surface. I saw landmasses with veins running through them, either rivers or the remnants of them as they made their marks traveling down to the sea. Cities were distinguishable because they looked as if someone had taken a shovel and turned up the ground. Agricultural lands had specific geometric shapes and were different colors depending on the crops and type of soil. I saw no real borders except the border between land and water. We humans have such conceit about how we've divided up the earth, but there is little evidence of it from space.

Most of our planet, I discovered, is covered by clouds. At first, I was disappointed, thinking I wouldn't be able to get good pictures, but I was soon entranced by the clouds. They have so many different shapes and formations. Sometimes, they looked like a thick, fluffy white blanket, and at other times like little scattered cotton balls. In some regions, they looked like someone had taken a paint brush, dipped it in white paint, and stroked it in different directions. It was as if God had used our lovely Earth as a canvas!

Seeing the clouds and their endless formations made me think of vacations with Hamid when we would lie outside and watch the clouds and announce what shapes we saw in them. I wished so much he could be with me on the station, enjoying the clouds. One day, Pasha saw me looking out the window in the service module and pointed at a big circular shaped cloud region and said, "Cyclone." The storm, a hurricane, was enormous, and I could sense its terrible, raw energy. I wondered if any humans were being pummeled while we soared peacefully above all its destructive power.

The best part was at night when I could see the stars. They were simply unbelievable. It was as if someone had spread diamond dust over a black velvet blanket. When I was supposed to be sleeping I put my head to the window and stayed there until the coldness of the glass gave me a headache. As I gazed out, I thanked God again for giving me this experience. I also thanked Him for letting my inner voice ring out through my blog, and I asked Him to give me the vision to see my path in life and the strength to pursue it. These were the most peaceful moments I had ever experienced in my life, and I felt a great source of positive energy. I had such a hard time sleeping because I kept forcing my eyes open to see the beauty and take it all in. Only a second longer, I would tell myself. Then I would tell myself the same thing again. And again.

As fascinated as I was with looking through the windows, I still kept a busy schedule aboard the station. Although I would have liked to have done more science experiments, the very short time I had to prepare didn't allow for much. Still, I did what I could. For the European Space Agency, I faithfully filled out a lower-back pain questionnaire. I also worked up a muscle atrophy study at the last minute with NASA astronaut and physician Mike Barratt. To gather data for this study, I took daily measurements of my arms, legs, waist, and chest. To ensure I was precise, I marked my body with black ink so I always measured at the same place. Applying a tape measure to oneself in zero-G requires contortions worthy of an Olympic gymnast. Misha came along and caught me measuring and said, "Are you crazy? Why are you working so hard? Enjoy yourself. You only have a limited time here. You have to make the best of it!"

I knew he was right, but my ingrained work ethic wouldn't allow me a complete holiday in space. I volunteered to fix dinner, cleaned up any messes I saw, and went around making certain the batteries in every camera were charged. I kept asking if there was anything else I could take care of, but the others were all so busy keeping to their schedules that they didn't have much time to think up things for me to do. L. A. and Pasha could often be seen with their heads in manuals and procedure books, preparing for the day when L. A. was to take over as commander of the station.

Although L. A. was always so serious about everything, and at first a little remote to me, I was happy that our time in quarantine had allowed us to become friends. Though it initially seemed we didn't have much in common, actually we did. We had both been born in other countries (L. A.'s birthplace was in Spain) and we had both made our way in the United States. It was true, however, that our paths since had been very different. I became an engineer and a successful businesswoman who often wore her heart on her sleeve. In contrast, L. A. had become a pilot, joined the military, and seemed to work to conceal his emotions as much as possible. Despite our differences, I valued his friendship. For his part, I think he was curious about me, often trying to figure out how my mind worked or why I lived the way I did. I hoped that we would stay in touch after we returned to Earth.

Because of our shared passion for science, education, and especially spaceflight, Thomas Reiter and I began a series of conversations—some might say friendly arguments—over our opposing viewpoints. He was a purist who was absolutely convinced the only way to advance in space was to have governments lead and control the way. Corporate intrusion into space, he said, would not work because pure science and the profit motive simply do not mix. I reminded him how commercial companies had accelerated advancements in medicine, computers, and materials while making the results more affordable and accessible. Private money, I went on to say, could more quickly accomplish great things in space than governments. After all, government space programs had plodded along for four decades, and space exploration was still terribly expensive and restricted to a very few people. I asked him, as a hypothetical, "Why not wear a Nike hat if Nike pays you enough money to develop a cure for diabetes?"

Thomas couldn't see it, replying that once he sold himself to the highest bidder, his research would be restricted to making a profit. I knew this was not true and cited many examples, but I couldn't convince him. When

I told him I believed the private sector would ultimately open up space for everyone, he insisted that space should be restricted only to dedicated scientists. In his opinion, to send people into space just for the experience was of no value. He smiled and said, "I don't mean you, Anousheh."

He did, of course, but he was trying to be nice about it. I argued that the only way to take great strides in space exploration was to make it more affordable. Governments wouldn't do it because they had no incentive. I gave him examples of what private money could do in areas like aviation, tourism, computers, and so forth. "Look," I told him, "ultimately we need to find a way for people to live and raise their families in space."

Thomas scoffed at this concept. "You've been watching too much *Star Trek*," he accused me, with some accuracy. "You know very well space is too harsh an environment for most people."

"So was the Wild West when people started moving there," I responded. "Or when the first little ships sailed across the oceans to get to the Americas. If they had stopped because of the dangers and the risks involved, imagine where we would be now?"

Our discussions would go on and on until we were both exhausted. None of our crewmates wanted to get involved. I'm certain I did not change Thomas's opinions nor did he change mine, but I savored our lively discussions and I think he did, too.

I continued my blog and went to the U.S. lab's laptop every night to work on it. I liked to write while everyone else was in bed. The station lights were dimmed for the sleep period and except for the white noise of the fans, it was quiet, so I could reflect peacefully on the events of the day and recall mental notes I'd given myself. I tried to write as if I were talking to Hamid or Atousa. The first time I decided to go through the ordeal of washing my hair in zero-G, I knew it would be fun to write about. It proved to be one of my most popular posts:

Well my friends, I must admit keeping good hygiene in space is not easy! There is no shower or faucet with running water. Water does not "flow" here, it "floats" ☺—which makes it a challenging act to clean yourself. So what do people do up here, specially the ones staying for six months at a time? They improvise!

There are wet towels, wet wipes, and dry towels that are used for cleaning yourself. Usually each person gets a wet towel a day and couple of dry ones. Now brushing your teeth in space is another joy. You cannot rinse your mouth and spit after brushing, so you end up rinsing and swallowing. Astronauts call it the fresh mint effect. ☺

The most interesting experience—or I should call it experiment—is washing your hair. Now I know why people keep their hair short in space. You basically take a water bag and slowly make a huge water bubble over your head and then very very gently, using a dry shampoo, you wash your hair. At the slightest sudden movement, little water bubbles start floating everywhere. I've made some video of my hair-washing experience that I will share when I return. ☺

Of course, water here is a valuable resource and is recycled, so anything wet is not thrown out, instead it is left out to air dry. There is a condensation collection unit that takes the moisture out of the air and recycles and purifies it. This includes sweaty clothes after exercising. One of the cosmonauts told me, "We are all very close to each other, we are like brothers and sisters; it is very unique because we drink each others' sweat." Now I know well what he means.

—Space Cadet Anousheh.*

---

* http://www.anoushehansari.com/blog/092506.php

Every morning, Russian mission control called and put Hamid on the line. He was always anxious to hear how I was doing and be reassured that all was well. I was also eager to hear his voice and hear that everything was under control back on Earth. The larger truth was I longed to feel his arms around me and wished so much that we could float in space together.

One morning, I overslept and missed Hamid's call. Knowing that he'd gotten up early to hear my voice, I felt awful. Pasha was in the service module and when he saw the distress on my face, he asked what was wrong. When I told him, he smiled benevolently and said not to worry. "You looked like you needed sleep," he said, "so I rescheduled you to talk to your husband on the next pass." I was so grateful to Pasha, I felt like hugging him. I didn't but, looking back on it, I think I should have.

Every other day or so, I used the IP phone to call Mom and Atousa. Each time I spoke to her, Atousa cried. I said, "Atousa, you have to stop this! I'm having the time of my life." She responded that she was crying out of happiness, but I'm not certain that was true. "I am coming home soon," I reassured her. "Don't worry." In contrast, Mom, after her bus-chasing episode, was now a rock, cheerful that her first-born was living her dream.

Around 6:30 p.m. each working day, we all gathered around the dining table in the service module, heated up a few cans of food or hydrated some freeze-dried meals, and shared stories. The others were all experienced space flyers and had more than a few tales to tell that always made me laugh. It was like being with a family and, in a very real way, we had already become one.

After months of eating the same fifteen basic meals, astronauts become very creative, mixing things together just to taste something different. Every so often, a special food package arrives aboard the shuttle or a *Progress* cargo ship. These "care packages," as they are called, often contained fresh food that has to be eaten the same day it arrives. You can imagine how good a fresh apple would taste after several months of canned food.

As with anything mechanical or electrical, there are occasional failures. On a closed system like the space station, depending on what breaks down, things can get very serious very fast. After the space shuttle had departed and just before we arrived, there was a minor emergency with the Russian-built *Elektron* oxygen generator. This device makes oxygen by a process of electrolysis of water laced with potassium hydroxide. Pasha, Thomas, and Jeff smelled something like burning rubber, and then saw smoke coming from the *Elektron*. When Pasha checked it, he found it too hot to touch and shut it down. Then he noticed a clear liquid drifting nearby and a sharp odor. After checking with the ground, he and the other two astronauts donned heavy rubber masks, pulled on rubber gauntlets, and carefully wiped up the liquid, which was probably water and potassium hydroxide that had escaped through a melted gasket. It was likely the gasket that had caused the smoke and burning odor. The contaminated wipes were then stuffed in a rubber bag, sealed and secured, and put inside the hab module of a docked *Soyuz* to be burned up later during reentry. It is critical that nothing toxic, no matter how small, be left in the atmosphere of the station; otherwise, it can be breathed into the lungs of an unsuspecting crew member.

As soon as we were on board, Pasha conferred with Misha and L. A. on the Elektron situation. Later, when some repairs were attempted on the device, I videotaped the work. L. A. asked if he could download the video for training and further analysis. I agreed and he forwarded it on to NASA. I heard later they were very appreciative and liked the fact I had made a record of the repair. It occurred to me that perhaps I should have asked Pasha and Misha if they agreed with this. After all, it was a Russian manufactured piece of hardware. When I mentioned it to Pasha and Misha, they just shrugged and told me not to worry about it. That was generally their answer to everything.

After several days of observation, I was amazed at how well everyone got along aboard the station. Much of that was due to good manners and simple courtesy. For instance, I observed that when a cosmonaut asked a question in English, his astronaut counterpart would often answer in Russian. The reverse was also true. It was done out of mutual respect. If only we had more people practice such courtesy on Earth, we would surely have a much more peaceful place to live. Of course, there were times when one of the crew would have a bad day and wouldn't be able to stand being around the others. The grumpy person would try to mask his feelings, and the others, who weren't really fooled, would do what they could to give him a little more space. It was remarkable when I really thought about it. There we were, six of us, in a place about the size of an average three-room house, filled with tons of equipment and with nowhere to go, yet we enjoyed being together.

⚜

A question that comes up frequently for every astronaut and cosmonaut is how he or she goes to the bathroom in space. Maybe it's because this is something we humans all have in common and, when we visit a foreign country, it is something we are all a little nervous about. In any case, here is what I know about tending to one's business in orbit.

At the time of my flight, there was only one toilet aboard the International Space Station. Located in the service module, it is of Russian design and manufacture. The design has been around for decades and was used first on the old Russian *Salyut* space stations, and then the more recent *Mir.* I have noticed the Russians have an engineering philosophy that encourages them to stick with what works, rather than strive for improve-ment. Likewise, in the United States, we have a phrase: "Better is the enemy of good enough." The practical meaning of this is that to improve a design that already works usually requires more time and money than the im-provement is worth. Of course, the value of an improvement is often sub-jective. In any case, as most of the users aboard the International Space Station can attest, the Russian toilet works most of the time, but we cer-tainly hope there will be improvements before space is opened to the vast majority of people.

What confronts the user of the station's toilet after sliding open its flimsy accordion door is a complex control panel of buttons and lights, a small seat, and a vacuum hose. Station residents are trained on the ground how to use the toilet because repair is difficult, time-consuming, and kind of nasty. The first time I used the toilet on orbit, I kept thinking, *Don't break it, Anousheh!* I even took the instruction manual inside with me for fear I would mess up.

Once inside the toilet, which is about the size of a bathroom on a stan-dard airliner, the accordion door is manually closed with a small magnet, al-though there are gaps all around the door, so there is not much real privacy. The next step involves the control panel. During each use, the correct but-tons and knobs on the panel must be pushed and turned in the prescribed order with the proper display lights indicating whether the procedure has been done correctly.

Once everything seems to be OK, it is time to get down to business. For urination, the vacuum hose has a funnel-shaped attachment that fits over, well, the place on the human body where, ah, the urine comes out. It is im-portant that this attachment fit correctly so that the vacuum does a thorough job. The urine is drawn into a chemical treatment tank that must be changed occasionally.

The next phase of business, euphemistically called "number two," is a bit more complicated. In a well beneath the seat (which looks like a standard toilet seat), there is a plastic bag. If all the knobs and buttons are configured correctly, fans create a light suction that pulls air through tiny perforations in the bottom of this bag. The space "goer" fits onto the seat using handholds for leverage and then, um, *goes.* The suction makes sure that everything ends up at the bottom of the bag. After a successful, er, voiding by the crewperson, the plastic bag with a built-in string at the top is removed, wet wipes are deposited, and the string pulled and tied off. Disposal requires the used bag to be pushed down the well on top of the other used bags. Then another bag is put into place, ready for the next user.

During these procedures, wet wipes are used to clean everything up, as it is exceedingly impolite to leave a mess for the next person. The residents of the International Space Station are fastidious in this regard. Thus ends my description of this very human requirement in space. May there be many improvements in the future!

✌⟡✵⟡✌

One thing I especially loved about space was the absence of gravity. It was amazing. Everything was effortless. I could lift a 500-pound block with one hand and move it around with one finger. I could do somersaults in the air. I recalled that as a child I had a recurring dream where, to the amazement of my family, I was able to fly from room to room. Now, even this dream had come true. If I wanted to move forward, all I had to do was lightly touch a wall or any other solid object with one finger and away I would go. If someone was blocking my way, I simply flipped over, grasped the handles on the walls, and propelled myself past. If I forgot my book at the other side of the module, I could ask someone closer to send it to me by giving it a nudge in my direction. It would fly across and land gently in my hand.

The first few days, I tended to push too hard, which would make me fly too fast, and—BANG!—I would hit a wall and bounce back to where I started. I was undeterred, however, and kept trying. Eventually, Misha complimented me on how skillfully I flew along the corridors and modules.

One day, Pasha and Jeff said they wanted to show me something. They put me in the middle of a node where I couldn't reach anything. They laughed as I realized I was stuck and, no matter how much I moved myself, couldn't go anywhere. After several minutes of struggling, the gentle breeze from a fan finally moved me close enough to a handle to grab it. I was laughing too hard to be mad at their little trick.

But weightlessness can also cause problems. For instance, I quickly learned that typing on a keyboard created a force strong enough to send me flying across the module. To compensate, there are bars all over the place for crews to hook their feet into and let them act as anchors. The day I arrived at the station, Pasha gave me some soft lambskin boots. I didn't know why and didn't wear them at first, but at night when I went to bed, I noticed the tops of my feet had small bruises and hurt like the devil. Then I realized what the boots were for. In space, you learn to use even your toes for leverage. It turns out the big toe is an especially powerful tool for astronauts. Who would have thought? It is a good thing we have not evolved away from the big toe. We may need it in the future.

Another aid in space is Velcro. It seemed as if everything on the station had Velcro attached to it—even us, on our coveralls. At first, I thought things could be secured by putting them in my pockets. But this worked only until I opened the pocket to take something out. Not only would that thing come out, but everything else along with it. It was so easy to lose things. Before long, I realized I had lost my lip gloss. I looked everywhere but I never did find it. I hope some future astronaut can use it!

My days and nights in space passed by. Even though I willed the clock to slow down it ticked relentlessly, unfazed by my wishes. All too soon, there would be only one day left, and then none, and then I would have to leave my lovely home in space and return to Earth. I tried hard not to think about the return. It would ruin the few days I had left. Instead, I tried to keep myself awake and make a vivid mental record of everything so that I would be able to savor it for the rest of my life.

✦✦✦

Back on Earth, the media kept calling me a "space tourist." Terri tried to get them to call me a "space ambassador," recognizing the international aspects of my background, but was only marginally successful. NASA Watch, an Internet space watchdog site, questioned the term, wondering who or what I was representing as an ambassador. Of all the descriptions used, I suppose I liked "space entrepreneur" the best. Not only did it reflect my business background, but it was also germane to what I hoped would be my future as a businesswoman—opening up the pathways of space for everyone. Later on, Keith Cowing, the editor of NASA Watch, wrote me a letter expressing his encouragement and support, which was very much appreciated. Actually, I didn't care what I was called. I was just happy to be in space.

Terri kept working hard to keep up with all of the requests for me to call from space. One interesting call was to the International Space University, which wanted to give me an honorary doctorate. Although Terri told the president of ISU that his remarks needed to be short in order to fit within the constraints of the communications satellite, his introduction was too long and the pass was complete before I could say a word! Terri worked diligently to set up another call but the same thing happened again. Happily, the third time was a charm; the president made his decree and I was able to express my gratitude from space.

To use the IP phone line on board the ISS required us to pay quite a lot of money to NASA, but even so, it was restricted to personal calls. I was not allowed to speak to the media on it or make any other kind of call, such as to ISU. For that kind of thing, I had to get permission from NASA or go back to the service module and use the Russian communications equipment, which was severely limited. Hamid wanted to announce we were making use of Prodea software when we used the IP, but NASA told us this was not allowed. This had to do with the fact that the American taxpayer had paid for this equipment and I was a private citizen on board the station as a "guest" of the Russians.

Since NASA controlled e-mail, every day I sent my blog entry to Terri for the Americans to review and censor. Terri told me not much was ever changed except for brand names. For instance, I wasn't allowed to say M&Ms. "Candy" was substituted instead. Once my blog entry was approved, Terri would post it on my Web site. She then went through the responses and sent a few of them to me, along with questions to answer. The heartfelt messages from my readers often made me cry.

When Terri wasn't struggling with space bureaucracies, schools, and university presidents, she took the time to send me some fun stuff, like a message that a local Texas radio station had voted me the hottest astronaut ever! I was bemused. All my life, I had tried to let the merit of my work speak for itself and not be marginalized because of my appearance. Yet here I was, accomplishing something really important, and all these radio guys could talk about was how I looked.

Return to Earth

On September 28, we had a schedule shift aboard the ISS that changed my wake-up time from 4 a.m. to 9 a.m. Since this was my last day on the station, I wasn't going to waste it sleeping. But from the moment I opened my eyes, I had butterflies in my stomach. In fact, I found I was in a state of complete distress. I was confused about what could possibly be causing this anxiety. It was only around 5:30 in the morning and no one was up, so I had nobody to talk to about how I felt. I eat when I'm nervous, and scavenged in the snack containers like a hungry cat. I ate cereal bars, cookies, dried fruit, almonds, and chocolate. During my binge, I thought to myself, *Anousheh, if you keep eating like this, you're going to have trouble fitting inside the* Soyuz!

Finally, unable to quiet my nerves, I went to the service module window and gazed at the Earth below. I felt an unbelievable positive surge of pure, benevolent energy. It occurred to me maybe it was being sent by everyone who had written me such happy and heartwarming messages while I was in orbit. It felt as if there was a strange warmth emanating from the blue-white glow of the atmosphere. I remembered then an ancient Persian tradition to celebrate the New Year. Our ancestors would jump over small fires while chanting, "Take away my yellow color and give me your red color!" In effect, they were asking the fire to take their weaknesses and return warmth, health, and strength. I felt like chanting the same thing, but what I wanted was to receive positive things without transferring anything negative to Earth. Sadly, it seemed there was already plenty of that to go around down there. I put on my iPod and listened to one of my favorite songs—"Fragile" by Sting—and watched a beautiful sea of clouds slide by. It didn't take long before I began to feel better. By the time the others woke, my distress had completely vanished.

Pasha had promised to help me set up the video camera so I could demonstrate some principles of physics using the stock of toys on board. Once everything was set up, Misha, Jeff, and Thomas participated in my video. I hoped it could be turned into a special program for the schoolchildren of the world. After I had finished interviewing them and my production was finished, it was time for lunch, and everyone gathered for a last meal together.

The discussion at the table centered on the fast-approaching time for Pasha, Jeff, and me to leave. Even though Pasha and Jeff were ready to go home and see their families, they were still nostalgic about leaving, since neither could be certain of ever going into space again. To cheer them up, I reminded them that one of my main goals for the future was to use private funding to build passenger spacecraft. I told them, "The best pilots for these flights will be former astronauts like you guys, so when you think of retiring, give me a call." They smiled appreciatively and said, "Sounds good!"

Before I knew it, it was time for us to go to the *Soyuz*. I was returning in a different capsule, since the one we flew up in was staying behind as a lifeboat. My new capsule was the one that had carried Pasha, Jeff, and Marcos to the station. My seat liner and space suit had already been moved to this vehicle and Pasha had also packed my stuff the night before. The habitation module was also crammed with garbage. During the last stages of our homeward flight, it was to be jettisoned to burn up in the atmosphere.

After a formal goodbye on camera, we had a teary-eyed farewell off camera with lots of hugs and kisses. Then, one happy cosmonaut, one happy astronaut, and one unhappy space entrepreneur got into the capsule and Misha, L. A., and Thomas closed the station hatch behind us. When we closed the *Soyuz* on our side, we saw a picture of the three of them waving good-bye taped to the inside of the lid. We all laughed, and our descent began with everyone in a good mood.

The next step was a painstaking check to make sure there were no pressure leaks between the hatches. That accomplished, we floated up inside the hab module, put on our space suits, and came back down to strap ourselves in. After another leak check, we were good to go. We got the go-ahead from mission control and began the lengthy procedures to undock. Suddenly, I felt so exhausted that I kept falling asleep. Seeing my eyes closed worried Pasha and he kept checking to make sure I was feeling OK. I answered, truthfully, "I don't know why I can't keep my eyes open. Sorry!"

Jeff had the best explanation: "You're coming off ten days of adrenaline rush. Your body is telling you it needs rest." He was probably right. I had been on a high during the entire experience and now I was on my way down in more ways than one. I felt a slight jolt when we undocked. I was sad to be leaving with no way to return. Would I ever come back? I could only pray that I would.

As Pasha backed us out, we had one last view of our dear home in the sky and then we turned away from the station to prepare ourselves for the descent. I had been advised by everyone who'd done it before that landing in a *Soyuz* was rough. When we got close to hitting the atmosphere, Jeff said, "Get ready. This is going to be a real roller coaster!" He reminded me to tighten my straps, and when the g-forces began to build, to tense my abdominal muscles. This would help keep the blood from draining from my head, which would cause a blackout. He said he would announce every stage of the descent to prepare me for what came next.

We fell into the atmosphere. At first, I felt and saw nothing unusual but then there was a big thump as the hab module was jettisoned. Almost immediately, an orange glow pulsed outside the window. It was our heat shield burning up. This was followed by a shower of sparks. It was like riding a shooting star. Pasha announced the G loads in Russian and Jeff translated it into English while giving me advice. "One point five Gs! Anousheh, are your belts tight as you can get them? Don't forget to use your stomach muscles!"

I was strapped down so tight it felt like the bones in my shoulders would break, but Jeff ordered me to pull them even tighter. "Two Gs!" he announced. "Get ready for more!"

I wish to advise all future *Soyuz* fliers that the Gs in the centrifuge feel like a lot less than the Gs on an actual descent. It felt as though an elephant had entered the capsule and was sitting on my chest. "Two point five!" Jeff announced, his voice as tight in his throat as my belts. "Two point seven! Two point eight! Three! Anousheh, are you OK?"

I was, but my face was being stretched in all directions. I squeezed my stomach muscles and tensed my whole body. It now felt like *two* elephants were sitting on my chest. I asked God to give me strength so I would not pass out. "Four point five Gs!" Jeff gasped. Then, "OK, now we're going down. Three point five, three point two, two point eight, one point five . . . OK, back to normal."

I smiled with relief until Jeff said, "Well, normal for a while. Parachutes next."

We had a few minutes of peaceful descent. Pasha asked how I was doing and I replied, "*Vsiyo kharashow*," meaning everything was fine. "Very good," he replied in English. Had he known Farsi, I'm sure he would have used that, too.

When we got close to parachute deployment, Jeff announced, "Here we go. Get ready!" I tensed every muscle in my body, then *ooomth!* The first parachute yanked us up and sent us into a crazy, violent spin. It felt like being on one of those saucers in an amusement park, only ten times more intense. I closed my eyes so I wouldn't get sick watching the instrument panel seemingly swirl around. The swinging and spinning slowed just as the big parachute deployed, causing us to gyrate again. Finally, everything stabilized.

The onboard computer automatically raised our seats for landing, making the small space in front of us even smaller. Jeff and Pasha counted down our descent from 3,000 meters to 200 meters and then, before they could give another reading, we struck the planet.

And I mean we struck hard; really, *really* hard. We hit the ground with such force I thought we had burrowed into the dirt. It felt like a million needles were suddenly plunged into my back. Then we bounced and rolled nearly upside down. With gravity pulling my back away from the seat liner, the needle sensation disappeared but I was still in some pain. Pasha checked to make sure we were all OK. Not wanting to admit my back hurt, I said everything was great and thanked him for a wonderful landing even though we were essentially hanging upside down.

I would later learn our capsule had landed in a desert area in Kazakhstan called Arkalic. When I peeked out the window, I saw the sun slowly rising over the horizon. It was still really hot inside the capsule from the heat of the reentry and I had sweat dripping from my face into my helmet. Then I smelled something like burnt wire and hoped the search-and-rescue team was on its way. Pasha announced the temperature outside was minus five degrees Centigrade. "Minus five!" I cried. "I want to go back to the station!"

Pasha and Jeff laughed and Pasha said, "No, no. Minus five is good!"

After a few minutes we heard a knock on the window. The search-and-rescue team was there. When they opened the hatch, the smell of crisp morning air flooded the capsule. I heard words of joy and congratulations in Russian. Pasha responded and laughed. Photographers pushed their lenses inside. Clicking, whirring cameras surrounded us.

We were handed hard covers to put over the instrument panels in front of us so we could step on them on our way out. Since Pasha was in the middle seat nearest the hatch, he was supposed to be the first out. With our straps so tight in our nearly upside-down position, his exit proved difficult. A search-and-rescue team member took out a knife and cut Pasha's knee straps, then after some grunting, managed to get his shoulder straps loose. Two men reached in, grabbed his arms, and pulled him out like a rabbit out of a hole.

Being in space is hard on your body. Your muscles grow lazy and have a difficult time acclimating to normal gravity. I was feeling this effect; my arms so heavy they seemed like they were made of lead, but this was no doubt mild compared to what Jeff and Pavel were feeling, since they had just spent six months in space.

After a minute or two of Jeff and me hanging in the *Soyuz,* a rescue team member returned and cut my straps. Because of the way the capsule had landed, I was higher than the others. The hatch lid was also in the way. My rescuer finally stretched his torso the width of the capsule so he could reach across the hatch and cut my knee straps and get me unbuckled. Then he tried to pull me out but I was stuck on something. Somehow, I managed to free myself. Many cosmonauts refer to being pulled from the capsule as a second birth. When I was drawn into the bright light of the new day, I understood why.

Outside, it seemed like mass confusion. There were so many excited people. They descended upon me, wrapped me in furs and carried me to a folding chair. Someone handed me a beautiful bouquet of roses and told me it was from the search-and-rescue team. There were cameras everywhere and the *click-click-click* of snapping pictures. Doctors kept leaning in, taking measurements, checking my pulse, and asking me how I felt. My nose was running and every so often, a nurse leaned in and wiped my face. It made me feel like a baby.

Someone handed me an apple but as soon as I started to take a bite, a doctor told me not to eat it. He was worried it would make me sick. The apple looked too good to resist and I started sneaking small bites. The nurse continued to wipe the sweat from my face and the apple juice from my chin—all in front of the cameras.

Jeff was the last one to be pulled from the capsule. After he was carried over and deposited beside me and Pasha, we all sat in our beach chairs while dozens of people milled around, chattering and shouting. The sun rose and I enjoyed feeling its warmth on my face. I wanted time to stop so I could have a moment to myself. I wanted to listen to the wind in the open desert of Arkalic and enjoy the dance of the clouds across the bright blue sky. Now that I had left the stars behind, I wanted to take in all the reasons why I should be happy back on Earth. I took a deep breath of the frigid air, closed my eyes, and put myself back where I really wanted to be, aboard the station. I could almost feel myself floating in my nook, watching the Earth slowly pass below. Then the reporters were unleashed upon us. When they started peppering me with questions, my peaceful image of space vanished.

I began to feel cold and wrapped myself tighter in the blanket. All of sudden, I heard a familiar voice behind me. "*Salam! Man omoudam!*" I couldn't believe my ears! It sounded like Hamid. I thought for a moment I was dreaming. I called out to him, "Hamid! Hamid!," but what I really wanted to say was, "Hamid, come and take me away from this place! Let's go somewhere safe and warm, away from it all! I want to hide in your arms!"

Even though I was not supposed to move my head very much, I looked up and saw it truly was Hamid bending over to give me an upside-down kiss. My heart filled with joy and I started crying as I reached up and touched his face.

"*Bargashti!* You returned!" Hamid cried.

Then he came around and knelt beside me. I reached out and held his hand as tightly as I could, not wanting to ever let go again. I realized at that moment that what I wanted more than anything in the universe, even more than being in space with the stars, was to be with my beloved Hamid forever and ever and ever.

You see? I told you this was a love story.

Epilogue

*I*f I had to describe myself after my wonderful flight into space and all that has come after, I would say I am a full-time entrepreneur and an ex-cosmonaut. My life is business, but my journey to space is never far from my thoughts. I know my brief visit to the stars changed me. Paradoxically, by leaving this world, I have become more connected to it and have a better sense of where I fit in it.

As entrepreneurs do, Hamid, Amir, Atousa, and I are once again pulling long hours, working far into the night, sleeping little, and arriving in our offices before the sun is up. I am happy in my work. I am happy because my dearest Hamid is with me, and because my wonderful sister, Atousa, and my ever-cheerful brother-in-law Amir are always nearby. I am happy because of my family. They are there to support me no matter what I want to do. My mother is so proud of me and Atousa and visits often. Aunt Chamsi still sends me gifts and encouragement. What amazing women they are, and how much I have learned from them!

Since my flight into space, my family has changed a bit. Atousa now has a beautiful son named Ilya, to whom I dedicated this book. He came into this world the day after Christmas in 2008. Sadly, Maman passed on to the next life shortly after my return from space. Yet in so many ways, she isn't gone at all. Like Buhbuh and Uncle Frank, she still guides me with her wisdom.

I'm pleased to report that I am in contact with most of the friends I made on my space journey. I was able to be there when Misha and L. A. landed in Kazakhstan after seven months in orbit. I greeted them with open arms, and to my joy, they were just as happy to see me. I've had the opportunity to see L. A. several times since. We have a special friendship based on our shared experience. L. A., whom I now call Mike, has even cooked for me and Hamid. Like everything he has ever tried his hand at, Michael Lopez-Alegria is a simply brilliant chef.

My days in orbit are still fresh in my mind. Sometimes at night in my bed, I imagine myself weightless again, my face pressed against the glass of my window, watching the world and the stars stream by. In a way, my space journey was like going to another dimension. Returning was a rapid descent back to what we think of as the real world. Like the confused people in science-fiction movies who accidentally time travel through wormholes, a return to Earth from space can be disorienting, as it was for me. Physically, I adjusted quickly. Emotionally, I was a mess. It took me months to find my place in what felt like a different world.

My breakthrough came when I accepted that my journey was not just *my* journey, but an experience that I was privileged to have and could not have had without the support of my family and so many others. I have also come to believe there was a reason why I went, a reason much greater than myself. I've spent countless hours on airplanes traveling all around the world to tell people that impossible dreams do come true and that they should never give up. I also tell them that space represents the future for all of us. These are things I profoundly believe.

Recently, I traveled to Jerusalem on behalf of an organization dedicated to peace. My first morning there, the city was alive with sounds—cars honking, a drill at a nearby construction site, birds chirping, and the Azan calling the Muslims to their midmorning prayer. I was enchanted. But when I visited both sides of the city, Palestinian and Israeli, reality set in. Along the border, it looked like a big prison, a prison where both sides were prisoners in different ways. One thing I learned during my years in Iran is that where there is no peace of mind, life is a prison. It was obvious in this city there was no peace of mind.

When I meet children, I grow optimistic. I always like to speak to young people, because I have faith in them. Their young minds are not hindered by artificial boundaries and they are willing to question everything. This is how progress occurs. When I visited a classroom on the Palestinian side of the border, the faces of the children were enthusiastic and in their eyes I saw a deep longing for what we think of in America or Europe as an ordinary life, one free of strife and war. I took a deep breath and told my story. I hoped they would see my journey as proof that even the most impossible dreams can come true. I told it all, from my childhood in Iran to how I came to United States and studied and worked until I succeeded. I told them how I had this dream to go to the stars and how it never died in my heart, how it was like a little glowing coal under ashes, waiting to come to life. Then I shared with them my trip to space. I told them that seeing Earth from up there had changed me and made me realize how we are all connected as human beings. I told them how determined I was to empower the youth across the globe so they could make our world a better place for their future.

I hoped I had made a connection with the children in that classroom. As I finished, I looked around the room and saw a sparkle in their eyes, a little glimmer of hope that maybe one day their dreams would also come true. I will never forget those eyes but there are many, many children out there desperate for hope. I want to give them that hope. As was written on my mission patch: *Imagine. Be the Change. Inspire.*

I wish every world leader could see what I saw from up there: one Earth, one planet, one home for all of us, the only thing separating us the seas, the only thing keeping us alive a thin, glowing blue atmosphere. If they flew into space and looked back, I cannot imagine they would do anything that would hurt people or our planet.

Occasionally I am asked, "Anousheh, with all your success and your trip to space, have you learned why we are here and what our purpose is?" I confess I don't know the answer. No one does. But my instinct and experiences tell me we are here to live life to the fullest and experience it with all our God-given abilities. That is what I have tried to do and what I wish for everyone.

And so my dreams live on, my passion for space continues unabated, and my willingness to work for peace grows with every day. One of my favorite poems is by Karen Ravn[*] and is perhaps an appropriate closing to this part of my story—a story not yet complete:

Only as high as I reach can I grow

Only as far as I seek can I go

Only as deep as I look can I see,

Only as much as I dream can I be.

---

[*]Karen Ravn's poem is reprinted here courtesy of Hallmark Cards, Inc.

Index